Creating A Curriculum That Works

A Guide to Outcomes-Centered Curriculum Decision-Making

Lorraine A. Ozar, Ph.D.

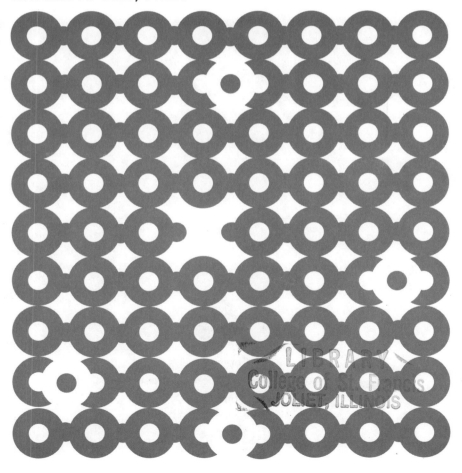

Acknowledgments

This book is the result of twenty years in the field. I am grateful to all the fine educators with whom I have been privileged to work in developing and refining this approach to curriculum decision-making. I have tried to provide references for all direct contributions. Some readers may recognize conversations and discussions we have had at workshops, conferences, breakfasts and dinners. For all these, thank you.

There are a few people who deserve special thanks for their help and support in completing this book. Thank you to my family, Dave, Kate, and Anne, for doing the laundry, going grocery shopping, cooking dinner and walking the dog so I could write; and most of all, for believing I had something worthwhile to say. Thank you to Leanne Welch, PBVM, and the many other SPC members who so warmly welcomed my workshop in St. Petersburg Beach and urged me to put it in writing, and who continued to support me throughout the process by sustaining enthusiasm for the project. Thank you to Elaine Schuster, Ph.D., Superintendent of Schools, Archdiocese of Chicago, for her understanding and support not only of this book, but of me as an educator and friend. Thank you to Bernie Bouillette, Ph.D., Headmaster of Loyola Academy, companion educator and friend, who supported my need to *really finish* the book even as I worked at learning a new job.

Thank you to the fine group of critical readers whose thoughtful comments and clear insights challenged me to write a much better book: Sr. Leanne Welch, PBVM; Mr. Don Miller; Sr. Mary Beth Kubera, D.C.; Ms. Janet Sisler; Ms. Cherie Casey; Ms. Janet Leitner; Sr. Mary Ann Governal; Ms. Mickey Lentz; Sr. Carol Ann Petersen, OSB; Br. Celestin Algero, SC; Dr. Robert Kealey; Sr. Regina Haney, OSF.

Finally, this book would never have made it to draft without the expert computer skills of Rosario Burger, who arranged all the figures in first form and corrected the final draft; thank you for staying with me from beginning to end.

I would also like to acknowledge the support and assistance of NCEA, particularly Frank Savage and Regina Haney, in bringing this book to its published form.

Contents

Foreword

The author of *Creating a Curriculum That Works*, Lorraine Ozar, Ph.D., was commissioned by the Supervision, Personnel and Curriculum (SPC) Advisory Committee to publish her invaluable curriculum design workshops.

The committee, a part of the Chief Administrators of Catholic Education (CACE) Department of the National Catholic Educational Association, provides a medium for interchange of ideas and discussion of issues related to personnel, curriculum and supervision. In light of current curriculum reform movements, the SPC Advisory Committee provides this tool, *Creating a Curriculum That Works*, for elementary and secondary educators in order to maintain excellence in Catholic schools.

The tool challenges Catholic educators to readjust their curriculum lenses to focus on results rather than tabulating time spent and lessons taught. As a result of implementing this guide of outcomes-centered curriculum, the focus shifts to the knowledge and skills students should accrue before graduating.

More important, Lorraine's work provides a means for Catholic educators to meet the challenges of the future as an *American Catholic School for the 21st Century*. Educators are invited to "champion superior standards of academic excellence in which gospel values and Catholic Church teachings are integrated in the lives and work of all members of our school community."

For these reasons, SPC is grateful to Lorraine for providing this invaluable tool for those Catholic educators committed to the *American Catholic School for the 21st Century*.

November 1, 1994

Sheila Durante, RMS
Chairperson
SPC Advisory Committee

Regina Haney, OSF
Assistant Executive Director
Chief Administrators of
Catholic Education

Chapter One

 **Identifying a New Approach to Writing Curriculum**

Writing Curriculum Is Hard Work

Most teachers and administrators would rather do almost anything other than write curriculum. It is the task that most easily accommodates all the daily crises and urgent requests that fill our schools. Teachers want to figure out what they will do with their students tomorrow, or for the week, and then do it. Yet, we will not be able to maintain the excellence Catholic schools are known for into the 21st century without writing new curriculum and writing it well.

There is widespread agreement in this country that grade school and high school education is failing a large percentage of our children and teens. While Catholic schools, in general, fare better than public schools on measures of achievement in basic skills (reading, language arts, mathematics), these "basic skills" are no longer enough.

The National Assessment of Educational Progress continues to underscore the shortcomings of graduates of our elementary and secondary schools, particularly in relation to the progress of students in other countries. The National Education Goals call for the achievement of world-class outcomes in English, mathematics, history, geography, and science. Forward looking corporations like Motorola include creative thinking, problem solving, interpersonal relations, teaming, organizational effectiveness and leadership in the list of skills and learning needed by *all* employees. Analysis of major trends shaping the world and reshaping schools points to the need for greater connectedness among traditionally discrete areas of learning and for stronger, richer partnerships between schools and the rest of the community, the rest of life. The National Congress on Catholic Schools for the 21st Century urged Catholic schools to move aggressively in providing an education that prepares students for living in a technological and global society, incorporates the contributions of men and women of diverse cultures and races, reflects the changing needs of family, church and society and challenges staffs, students and parents to reject racism, sexism and discrimination.

Catholic schools, just as public schools, can no longer rely on "business as usual" to insure excellence for the 21st century.

1) We must be as willing and able to demonstrate achievement in creative problem solving and collaboration as we are now willing to demonstrate achievement in reading and mathematics.

2) We must be even more astute and purposeful than we have been in seeing to it that the transformational values of our mission and philosophy concretely shape day-to-day teaching and learning.

3) We must find even more effective and compelling ways for the integration of faith, life, and learning to permeate the actual curriculum for every student.

This book offers an approach to curriculum decision-making aimed at helping our schools to become and/or remain *values-based, learning-centered* communities for the *21st century*. The book is written to be used by local schools—teachers, principals, parents—to establish the framework and common vision necessary to design and implement a curriculum that consciously connects mission and philosophy, discipline-specific standards, and knowledge about teaching and learning.

The main problem with most curriculum in schools today is that it focuses on content rather than on learning. Consider the effect of focusing on the quality of materials and parts in a car with little concern for how the car drives in actual road conditions. Consider the effect of concentrating on the ingredients in a recipe and the quality of cooking utensils, with little concern for the taste and appearance of the final dish. Consider the effect of emphasizing specific plays and fine execution of distinct maneuvers without careful attention to how the plays and maneuvers come together in a team's winning or losing the game. Students learn content, but it is not the whole, or even the heart, of the learning.

The outcomes-centered curriculum decision-making process outlined in this book helps schools generate curriculum focused on learning. It rests on the conviction that educators have three things to do:

1) Identify what is the significant learning.

2) Design valid ways for students to demonstrate the significant learning.

3) Find ways to help the significant learning happen better, richer, quicker and safer than on the street.

The curriculum we design is no more than a good road map for doing these three things harmoniously in actual classrooms with actual students.

There is no simple formula for building such a curriculum. Each school must build its own. But the success of the process rests heavily on achieving a common vision of what a curriculum focused on significant learning must provide and how the major pieces of such a curriculum fit together.

Curriculum that focuses on significant learning begins with clearly articulated learning outcomes. Graduation outcomes articulate the broadest, richest, most integrated learning that a school commits to for its graduates. At this level, outcomes will be interdisciplinary, multi-dimensional, value-laden and connected to real life. In the development of a school's curriculum, graduation outcomes shape the more discipline-specific (subject area) outcomes, which in turn shape outcomes for courses, grade levels and units.

Once a school formulates the significant learning outcomes that will drive the curriculum, local educators must then design a wide range of assessments that give students the opportunity to demonstrate the learning specified by the outcomes. Finally, teachers will select a variety of teaching strategies and learning activities that will most likely promote the learning stated in the outcomes and demonstrated in the assessments.

This process works. When schools design curriculum by first deciding what constitutes significant learning for this piece of instruction (unit, course, grade/cluster, multi-year sequence, graduation), and then by designing assessments and strategies to match, more learning occurs for more students. The broader and more integrative the outcomes, the more multifaceted the assessments must be, and the more dynamic and creative the strategies we must use.

The examples of curriculum that connect outcomes, assessment, and teaching/learning strategies in this book use outcomes on many levels: graduation, subject area, course, unit, and occasionally lesson. Our ultimate goal in building a curriculum focused on significant learning must be to consciously use the broader, more integrative *graduation* outcomes and reality-based *subject area* outcomes as reference points for more immediate course, grade/cluster, and unit curriculum decisions. However, sometimes teachers can see more clearly how the connections in an outcome-centered curriculum work by first making these connections closer to their immediate teaching.

Developing curriculum that focuses on significant learning is the work of a *community:* teachers, administrators, parents, other professionals and society. The process is messy and ambiguous, as well as stimulating and rewarding. No one will find himself or herself completely in tune with all the examples and samples in this book. Good. I would act contrary to my deepest beliefs about real curriculum development were I to offer any one item as *the best way* to do this or that. Some sections of the book may appear repetitious—saying the same thing from slightly different perspectives. Good. Skim what you already understand; consider it again with different emphasis to feel more comfortable with your own processing of the material.

This book will be successful if local school communities use it to do two things: 1) come to a common understanding of the three essential pieces of a curriculum that focuses on student learning (outcomes, assessments, and strategies); and 2) agree on how these pieces *must work together* to increase learning. Then write it down in a way that makes sense for your school. Your written curriculum may or may not resemble any of the formats presented in this book. The value of an example lies in the product it stimulates, not in the example itself.

Finally, let me offer eight principles that underlie this approach to creating a curriculum that works and which I will use to organize sections of the book:

Principles of Outcomes-Centered Curriculum Decision-Making

Principle 1:   Shift the focus to an *output* mindset.

Principle 2:   Significant learning *outcomes* provide the *foundation* for a curriculum that works.

Principle 3:   Select outcomes that touch both the *values-integration* plane and the *discipline-specific* plane.

Principle 4:   View the curriculum you will build as a concise statement of the *matches* you want among outcomes, assessments, and strategies.

Principle 5:   In the written curriculum, whatever the format, specify *enough and not too much.*

Principle 6:   Outcomes and assessments *together* form the basis of a curriculum that works.

Principle 7:   Strategies that respect the *natural functioning of the brain* will result in more significant, longer-lasting learning.

Principle 8:   *All* areas of the curriculum, including religious education and values formation, benefit from outcomes-centered curriculum decision-making.

Chapter Two

 Defining Key Terms

Defining a Learning Outcome

The best way I have found to define a learning outcome is as an answer to the question, "What should students be able to do when they leave that they couldn't do when they came?" We can ask the question after eight or nine years of elementary school or four years of high school. (**Graduation Outcomes**) We can ask it after eight years of language arts or four years of high school English. (**Program Level Outcomes**) We can ask it about a single subject on a grade/cluster level or a single course. (**Grade Level/Cluster** or **Course Outcomes**) We can ask the question about a unit or a lesson. (**Unit Outcomes, Lesson Outcomes**) Although the answers may vary, the question remains the same. What should students be able to do at the end of this period of instruction that they couldn't do at the beginning?

All too frequently, the words *goal, outcome* and *objective* are used interchangeably in professional literature and sample curriculum. This lack of precision muddies the waters and makes the business of writing curriculum much harder and less productive. **Figure 2.1** presents a visual representation of the relationship among the three. A *goal* is a general statement of purpose or intent. By its very nature, a goal is broad and difficult to observe directly, hence the amoebic shape. An *outcome* is more defined, like a clear rectangle, and stated from the student's point of view. It tells us what students will *do* and thus points to observable behavior. What students should "know" and "be like" are also expressed in observable behavior and are meant to be included in the more comprehensive statement, "what students will *do*." An *objective* is in the same family as an outcome because it tells what students will *do*; however, it is more specific, encompassing a smaller period of instruction (smaller rectangle with dimensions). **Figure 2.2** provides three sets of examples of educational goals, outcomes and objectives.

Before examining these samples, let me make one further comment on terminology. The approach to curriculum decision-making presented in this book rests on making a clear differentiation between goals on the one hand and outcomes/objectives on the other. Essentially, *outcome* and *objective* fit the same definition (what will students be able to *do* as a result of instruction), but in relation to different scope of subject matter and/or time. The term "outcome" usually refers to larger, more inclusive statements of learning (graduation, subject area, grade level/cluster, course outcomes); whereas the term "objective" usually refers to less inclusive, more concrete state-

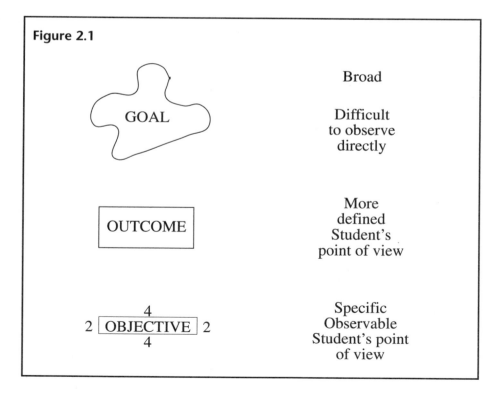

Figure 2.1

GOAL

Broad

Difficult
to observe
directly

OUTCOME

More
defined
Student's
point of view

4
2 | OBJECTIVE | 2
4

Specific
Observable
Student's point
of view

ments of learning (unit objective, lesson objective). The term "outcome" may be used in reference to smaller periods of instruction if desired, such as "unit outcomes".

Using the first example in **Figure 2.2**, a school might have as an important goal for science instruction that students understand the impact of science on their lives. Stated as such, this goal is not helpful in curriculum decision-making. It may sound good on paper or make us feel good about our intention to make science education meaningful to students. It may even comprise an accurate description of an important thrust of the school's science program, but it does not tell us what to look for if the goal is achieved. We cannot observe students "understanding the impact of science on their lives." And because this statement does not tell us what to look for in students, it fails as a useful tool in making decisions about what to teach, how to teach it and how to know when students have learned.

Figure 2.2	Examples
Goal:	Understand the impact of science on their lives.
Outcome:	Students will be able to use relevant scientific concepts and procedures in daily life.
Objective:	Students will be able to apply principles of energy conservation to make decisions about energy issues in their own homes.
Objective:	Using the principles of energy conservation, students will take a stand on current political issues involving energy and be able to defend their position.
Goal:	Life-long fitness
Outcome:	Students will develop habits which contribute to life-long fitness.
Objective:	Students will be able to establish realistic personal fitness goals.
Objective:	Students will be able to explain the role of warm-ups and cool down periods before and after strenuous activity.
Objective:	The students will be proficient to the point of enjoyment in at least one individual leisure time sport.
Goal:	Increase imaginative thinking.
Outcome:	Students will develop and communicate imaginative and inventive ideas.
Objective:	Students will be able to use visual language to describe objects and to explain ideas.
Objective:	Students will be able to work independently and in small groups to produce original visual images.
Objective:	Given an open-ended question or problem, the student will generate at least three plausible responses and communicate one response in a visual medium and in writing.

Transforming this goal into an outcome statement takes us much further: students will be able to use relevant scientific concepts and procedures in daily life. This statement is still very broad, but it begins to point us in a direction of what to look for if learning is happening. It begins to give us a basis for inclusion and exclusion of teaching/learning activities, materials and assessment tools. If, in pursuit of the goal of students' understanding the impact of science on their lives, a school states as an outcome of science instruction that students will use relevant scientific concepts and procedures in daily life, then a number of important things about the science curriculum become true:

1) science instruction cannot consist entirely in the communication and recall of information;

2) students must engage in application activities;

3) students must have opportunities to discover and demonstrate connections between science knowledge and their own experiences.

The two objectives in this set of examples help us even more. In a specific science course, grade level science program or a unit within either of these, the two example objectives communicate more precisely what to look for if the desired learning has occurred. Both objectives take the outcome —application of scientific knowledge to current experience—and specify the looked-for behavior in terms of concrete subject matter.

Specifying the unit objective, "students will be able to apply the principles of energy conservation to make decisions about energy issues in their own homes," a seventh grade science teacher has some very clear criteria for curriculum decision-making:

1) the unit must include knowledge of the principles of energy conservation;

2) students must engage in activities in which they apply these principles to situations in their homes, school, neighborhood;

3) students must practice decision-making that builds on the principles studied in class;

4) students must have an opportunity to present some decision of their own and connect it to principles of energy conservation.

Given these parameters established by the objective, the teacher has a sound basis concentrated on student learning for selecting appropriate teaching/learning activities, materials, assignments and assessments. Equally important, if the objective is a good one, using it as the basis for selecting teaching/learning strategies and for designing effective assessment tools makes it much more likely that there will be a match among what teachers expect, what they teach, and what they evaluate. Such a match creates powerful learning.

We can make the same kind of analysis of the second objective in this set of examples: "using the principles of energy conservation, students will take a stand on current political issues involving energy and be able to defend their position." A high school science teacher who articulated this statement as one of the course objectives for physical science would also find tremendous help in curriculum decision-making based on student learning. Not only would the course include knowledge and understanding of the principles of energy conservation, but also knowledge and understanding of current political issues related to energy conservation, opportunities for students to make connections between scientific knowledge and current affairs, practice in forming judgments based on sound reasons and opportunity to present persuasive arguments. The teaching/learning strategies likely to promote mastery of this objective would necessarily go beyond the standard lecture, textbook reading and question/answer drills. Further, the assessment needed to measure performance of the objective could not remain in the form of an information-focused test alone.

The outcome and the objectives promote the goal—understanding the impact of science on their lives. But stated in terms of what *students* will *do* to evidence learning, they also provide teachers and administrators with a clear, readily communicable basis for making decisions about what to teach, how to teach it, and how to know when students have learned.

Schools could develop many other outcomes for each of the goals in **Figure 2.2**. Likewise, many different objectives would contribute to achievement of the sample outcome. Formulating the "right" set is the first task of outcomes-centered curriculum development as presented in this book.

Moving from Goals To Outcomes

In a well-aligned curriculum, one with a high degree of congruence among the written, tested and taught curriculum, we should be able to observe a connection between the teacher's day-to-day choices and the school's overall philosophy and graduation outcomes. **Figure 2.3** presents two examples of such alignment.

In the first example, the philosophy of this elementary school includes the statement, "Students will be participating citizens in an increasingly interdependent world." This statement is akin to an educational *goal* as defined earlier in this chapter and as such is difficult to translate directly into teaching/learning decisions; however, it does represent an important direction in the educational program of this school. So, for the diploma to truly reflect the accomplishment of the school's educational goals, the fac-

---

Figure 2.3

Alignment by Way of Outcomes/Objectives
1. Philosophy Statement
2. Graduation Outcomes
3. Subject Area Outcomes
4. Grade-level Subject Outcomes/Course Outcomes
5. Unit Objectives
6. Lesson Objectives

Examples at each level:

1. Students will be participating citizens in an increasingly interdependent world.
2. Students will be able to connect knowledge with beliefs and actions.
3. Students in grades K-8 will be able to make decisions and justify them in relationship to democratic principles. (Social Studies)
4. Students will identify their own responsibilities in the communities of which they are members. (Grade 3 Social Studies)
5. Students will compare responsibilities of residents of a town and members of a small group like a class or family.
6. Students will list jobs that must be done for people to live together in a community.

---

1. Students will live a productive life in a changing world.
2. Students will use effective critical thinking skills.
3. Students will become adept in using scientific method in problem solving. (Science)
4. Students will draw correct inferences supported by laboratory data. (Course Outcome Biology)
5. Working from selected slides, students will be able to account for the condition of the observed cell.
6. Students will correlate the slide of a specific cell with the appropriate phase of cell division.

ulty and administration of this school must translate the goals inherent in the philosophy into a curriculum that can be communicated and delivered. Using student learning outcomes and objectives to do this is the best way to insure that individual teacher decisions match and promote the important educational goals of the school.

Translating Goals into Curriculum

Let's consider how a school might use learning outcomes and objectives to translate this goal—participating citizens—into a communicable and deliverable curriculum. The faculty would first consider the question, "What would students, as participating citizens in an increasingly interdependent world, be able to do?" One answer: they would be able to connect knowledge with beliefs and actions. The next step involves connecting this graduation outcome to the subject areas taught in the school.

In social studies, for example, what would students do to demonstrate that they are able to connect knowledge of social studies with beliefs and actions? One answer: students will be able to make decisions and justify them in relationship to democratic principles. Both the graduation outcome and the social studies outcome are very broad statements, but they begin to point teachers in a direction of what to look for if learning consistent with the goal is happening.

Moving to the grade level, a third grade social studies teacher operating in this model asks, "What would students in third grade social studies do to show that they are moving towards making decisions and justifying them in relationship to democratic principles? One answer, consistent with the subject matter of third grade social studies in this school, could be that students will identify their own responsibilities in the communities of which they are a member. At this point, the specific grade three social studies outcome begins to provide clear direction for curriculum decision-making. Unit and lesson objectives consistent with this grade level outcome provide even stronger support for selecting teaching/learning strategies, materials and assessment tools.

If these sample outcomes and objectives were part of the written curriculum of a school, the third grade social studies teacher whose students accomplished the stated lesson, unit, and grade level outcomes would be contributing directly to their mastering one of the significant educational goals of the school—participating citizens. Because the school's written curriculum includes grade and unit level outcomes, the teacher would not need to continually question the connection between day-to-day teaching and graduation outcomes. Rather, the teacher could focus his creative energy on selecting the most appropriate activities and materials to help *this* group of students achieve the learning.

The outcomes and objectives provide the teacher with clear criteria for deciding what to teach, how to teach it, and how to know when students have learned. In addition, decisions made on the basis of the stated outcomes and objectives assure the teacher that what's going on in her classroom really matches and promotes the significant educational goals of the school. In a well aligned curriculum, the answer to the question, "Why are you doing this in your classroom" is virtually always, "because it promotes achievement of the significant learning articulated in the outcomes/objectives."

The second set of examples in **Figure 2.3** describes the same sort of decision-making process in a high school curriculum. The school translates the philosophy statement, "Students will live a productive life in a changing world," into a graduation outcome that begins to describe what students will do if they are accomplishing this important educational goal. In this case, one thing students would be able to do if they were reaching this graduation outcome is use effective critical thinking skills.

In turn, the science department asks what students would do as a result of science instruction to demonstrate that they are using effective critical thinking skills. Thus, a department outcome could be "become adept in using scientific method in problem solving." A course outcome for biology that contributes to students' becoming adept in using scientific method in problem solving states that "students will draw correct inferences supported by laboratory data." Similarly, the unit and lesson objectives promote mastery of course, department and, ultimately, graduation outcomes by specifying what students will do to demonstrate learning in terms of increasingly specific subject matter.

As in the first set of examples, articulating this school's curriculum in terms of graduation, department, course and unit outcomes and objectives provides a solid basis for day-to-day teaching decisions that are much more likely to contribute to the significant learning identified in the mission and philosophy of the school.

Summing It Up

Formulating a written curriculum based on learning outcomes and objectives means a lot of work at the outset. Having such a curriculum in place saves tremendous time and energy in the long run *and* assures teachers and administrators that what is actually being taught and learned matches what the school declares to be important learning. Teachers must make decisions every time they set foot in the classroom. Making them on the basis of carefully arrived at and periodically reviewed learning outcomes does not happen *in addition to* other decision-making tasks and processes already in place, but *instead of* these other, less effective curriculum processes.

Chapter Three

 ## Shifting Focus from Input to Output Mindset

Principle 1: Shift the focus to an output mindset.

Ask any educator what he wants most and almost always he unhesitatingly replies, "I want my students to learn more and I want more of my students to learn." Increasingly, educators are becoming convinced that using learning outcomes as the basis for curriculum decision-making holds the most promise for realizing the goal of increased learning for all students. Why, then, doesn't more school curriculum reflect an outcomes-centered approach?

As in other areas of personal and professional life, what we do is determined by our frames of reference, by the existing mindset that shapes the questions we ask, the data we observe, the alternative actions we consider. The prevailing mindset in schools across the United States can be characterized by what I call an input model. With an input model, the focus rests on what we, the educators, put into the learning situation. Traditional school evaluation processes operate from this mindset. They ask, "Do we have what it takes to produce a quality educational program?"; "Do we have certified teachers?"; "Do we have enough books in the library?"; "Do we have a written curriculum?" They presume, of course, that if we have the right pieces in place, learning will happen.

From this focus, teachers begin curriculum design with these questions: "What shall I teach?" and "What shall I cover?" Faced with a new grade, course or material to teach and fit into a unit, teachers usually begin by asking these input model questions to help them determine what *they* will do, what *they* will put into the classroom.

We will get much better results in student learning if we shift our focus to an output model. With an output model, we begin curriculum decision-making with two quite different questions: "What shall students learn?" and "How will I know they've learned it?" As we shall see, this one change of perspective has a profound impact and compelling results.

When teachers begin with the second set of questions, the answer to the question "What shall I teach?" reflects what it is we want students to learn rather than what we want to teach. The student and her need to live creatively and productively in a democracy, in a church or on the earth become the driving force and the touchstone of accountability for what we do, not an individual teacher's background, experience, and personal preference. In other words, significant learning outcomes, identified by the community of educators and others, set the parameters for teacher decisions. Individual teacher experience and preference shape day-to-day creativity in the classroom *within the context* of the agreed upon learning outcomes.

Let me give you some examples of the difference this shift in focus makes. Here are some goals from actual curriculum guides:

- To understand the nature and purpose of government

- To understand the genetic continuity of life

- To understand an essay and how it is put together

- Ventures into space

In an input model, the teacher approaching teaching any one of these areas begins by asking, "What should I teach and what should I cover? If we're going to study the nature and purpose of government, what should be included? What are the key concepts, points of information? What materials are available? What have I done that's worked before?" The materials and strategies chosen would be very teacher-centered, driven in large part by the teacher's background and experience; they would be potentially different from the methods selected by the teacher next door and, perhaps, different from the declared educational goals of the school. The teacher would teach the materials selected, using the strategies selected and then test what was taught. There would be no basis for critiquing the results other than the students' performance on tests developed by the teacher to see if students got the material. Looking at student performance on tests with an input focus can tell us only whether students "got" what the teacher taught; it cannot tell us whether what they "got" was enough.

Taking the same subject matter and approaching curriculum decision-making with an output focus, the teacher begins by asking, "What should students be able to do as a result of instruction about and interaction with the subject matter called nature and purpose of government?" Depending on the answer to that question, the teacher selects teaching strategies, learning activities and assessment tools that would facilitate the outcome.

What would students who "understand the nature and purpose of government" be able to do? Here are three possible outcomes:

1) Students will state and explain information presented in class about the nature and purpose of government.

2) Students will write a constitution for a new nation.

3) Students will participate actively and effectively in student government or local government over the course of the year.

In an output model, teachers use these answers to the initial question as the starting point for curriculum decision-making. In other words, if this is what students should be able to do after instruction on the nature and purpose of government, what kinds of assessments will I need to use to let them demonstrate the learning and what kinds of teaching strategies and learning activities will most likely promote the desired learning?

Using the first outcome as a starting point would probably result in a social studies curriculum like many we know: read text, listen to teacher presentation, take notes, engage in question/answer sessions, discuss major points, complete worksheets and, finally, pass an objective test on the information. Not very exciting or challenging, but at least this statement of what students will learn gives the teacher some basis on which to choose what will or will not be part of the learning experience. Once the school has identified the information to be learned, the teacher must devise assessments and teaching/learning activities that lead students to state and explain it.

With the second outcome as the starting point, the curriculum needs to be very different. For one, the assessment could not be an objective test.

Likewise, preparing or coaching students to demonstrate mastery of this outcome by writing a constitution for a new nation necessitates opportunities for them to process information about government concretely. They would need to analyze, predict consequences, generate hypotheses and make decisions. Probably, the results would be better if students worked in groups or talked to each other about their own thinking and processing. This second statement of what students will learn also gives the teacher a clear basis on which to choose what will or will not be part of the learning experience. Because the second outcome represents richer, more significant learning, it challenges the teacher to select richer, more significant assessment tasks and richer, more engaging teaching/learning strategies as the only likely ways to prepare students to demonstrate the learning.

When we state curriculum in the language of goals, the teacher remains on his own to decide what this means in terms of level of learning and concrete decisions in the classroom. For one teacher, it might mean that students will define the terms and use them to fill in the blanks on a short answer test. For another, it might mean that students will put the concepts into practice by acting in a simulated or real-life government or writing a constitution for a new nation. Who is right? And on what basis will we decide which learning better matches the school's vision as stated in the mission, philosophy, and graduation outcomes? More often than not, no one asks which learning is preferred. We accept the input model and let each teacher focus on answering the question "What shall I teach?" Teachers may answer this question based on an implicit sense of what they think students should learn, but implicit and vague connections often lead to inequities among classes and less effective teaching and learning.

Any outcome designed around learning rather than teaching is a step in the right direction. *Good* outcomes can be tremendous catalysts for increasing learning and improving teaching.

We could follow a similar pattern of analysis with curriculum stated in topical language, for example, Ventures into Space. If I am a fourth grade teacher presented with the curriculum guide shown in **Figure 3.1**, on what basis will I decide what learning activities to design, what teaching strategies to use, what assignments to give, what resources to access, what field trips to take, what evaluations to use? Probably, I'll follow the textbook. Maybe I'll skip the hands-on projects because there isn't enough time or space or materials or because these students don't seem mature enough. Or maybe because I'm uncomfortable with noise and movement in class (or I judge my principal is). As long as the students can pass the end of chapter test, that's enough.

But is it? What if the school philosophy talks about active learning, higher order thinking and initiative? What impact does that have on the way I teach Ventures into Space?

In an output model, the first step in curriculum planning is to translate the curriculum topic into learning statements or outcomes. What will students be able to do who have achieved the intended learning on this topic? Three possible outcomes for Ventures into Space:

1) Students will name the major space exploration missions launched by the United States.

2) Students will assess the effectiveness of the United States space program.

3) Students will forecast applications of space exploration in the year 2010.

If being able to name space exploration missions constitutes learning, then the end-of-chapter test might be enough to assess learning and hands-

---

Figure 3.1

4th Grade Science

Goal: To use scientific knowledge in comprehending the impact of science and technology on the individual, culture, and society through study of such topics as:

1. Energy production and use.
2. Jobs and careers.
3. Natural resource use and management.
4. All living organisms within populations.
5. Various modes of transportation.
6. Weather modifications.
7. Genetics.
8. Chemical development and usage.
9. Methods of communication.
10. The amount, control and usage of pollution.
11. Use and/or misuse of land.
12. Ventures into space.
13. The ability of species to survive.
14. Design and usage of computers.

on projects won't be required. If learning Ventures into Space means assessing the effectiveness of the U.S. space program or forecasting applications in 2010, resources beyond the textbook will be needed and hands-on projects will play a central role in the curriculum. Once again, if teaching decisions are to be effective in promoting the intended learning, the selection and design of teaching strategies, learning activities, and assessment tools will need to vary depending on which of these learning outcomes the school selects. Topical statements of curriculum, like goal statements, provide no clear basis for curriculum decision-making. Outcomes, as statements of intended student learning, do provide a clear basis for selecting teaching/ learning strategies, materials, assessment tools, etc.; the stronger and more appropriate the outcomes, the more powerful and potentially effective the resulting curriculum.

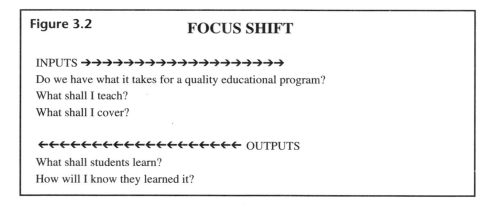

Figure 3.2 **FOCUS SHIFT**

INPUTS →→→→→→→→→→→→→→→→→→→→
Do we have what it takes for a quality educational program?
What shall I teach?
What shall I cover?

←←←←←←←←←←←←←←←←← OUTPUTS
What shall students learn?
How will I know they learned it?

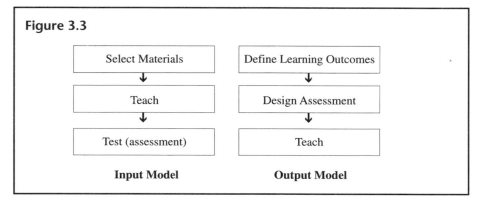

Figure 3.3

Select Materials	Define Learning Outcomes
↓	↓
Teach	Design Assessment
↓	↓
Test (assessment)	Teach
Input Model	**Output Model**

Figure 3.2 illustrates the shift in focus required for outcomes-centered curriculum decision-making. **Figure 3.3** represents this shift in terms of the decision-making flow used by teachers.

In the first decision-making flow, teachers faced with a new teaching situation usually begin by examining available materials. They ask, "What's the textbook? What have I used that might work? What have other teachers used?" Once they select materials, teachers in this input model teach the materials and then test what they've taught.

In an output model, the decision-making flow changes. Faced with a new teaching situation, teachers begin by defining the learning: What should students be able to do as a result of instruction in this subject matter? The resultant learning outcome is from the student's point of view and is observable. The second decision the teacher makes, *before ever setting foot in the classroom*, is to design the assessment tool she will use to let the students demonstrate achievement of the learning. Only in the third place does the teacher then select teaching strategies/learning activities that she will use to coach the students to fine performance on the assessment. Does this mean the teacher's job is to teach to the test? Absolutely YES, assuming that the "test" has been designed as a valid indication of achievement of the out-

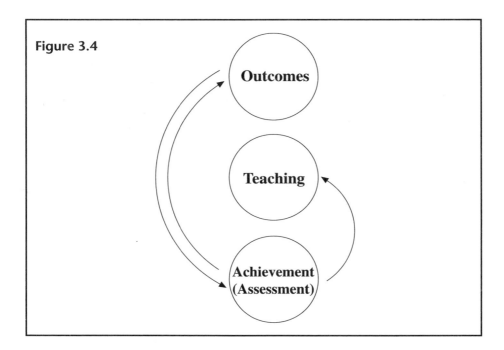

Figure 3.4

come. (Assessment is a better term in this context because it suggests a variety of performances beyond the paper and pencil kinds we usually associate with "test.")

Figure 3.4 diagrams the relationship among outcomes, assessments and teaching in yet another way. Outcomes and achievement (determined by assessment) represent the before and after of the same thing. Teaching belongs in the middle as the mediation between the desired learning (outcome) and the demonstrated learning (achievement). Assessment, here, refers to whatever opportunity teachers use formally for the learner to demonstrate learning. Teaching refers to the whole mix of input selected by the teacher to facilitate and promote learning: materials, strategies, field trips, outside resources, learning activities, etc.

In outcomes-centered curriculum decision-making, educators ask and answer three questions *in this order*:

1) What is the significant learning to be achieved ? (Outcomes)

2) How will students show they have achieved it? (Assessment)

3) What will teachers do to help it happen? (Strategies)

Summing It Up

In other words: articulate outcomes; design assessments to match; and teach so that students perform well on the assessments. The teaching decisions come last. **Establishing both outcomes and valid assessments before making practical teaching decisions will result in richer, more effective learning and teaching.** This is the basic message of this book. Several root assumptions, of course, ground the message, namely, that the outcomes are *significant*, the assessments are *valid and authentic*, and student performance is used as *feedback* to reinforce and/or alter teaching strategies.

Chapter Four

 **Writing Outcomes**

Principle 2: Significant learning outcomes provide the essential foundation for a curriculum that works.

A student learning outcome has two fundamental characteristics: 1) it is stated from the *student's* point of view, and 2) it indicates *observable* behavior. Consider the following statements:

- To become aware of computer applications in math

- To know the periodic table

- To appreciate the plays of Shakespeare

- To study Spanish speaking cultures

- To foster a love of neighbor

- To understand the Bill of Rights

None of these are outcomes. We cannot observe students becoming aware of computer applications, knowing the periodic table, appreciating the plays of Shakespeare or understanding the Bill of Rights. They must *do* something observable to show us that in fact they do understand, know, appreciate, or are aware. Likewise, "to study Spanish speaking cultures" says nothing about what students will *do* to indicate that learning has occurred. Do we observe them reading books? making maps? watching movies? listening to lectures? Do any of these observations indicate that *learning* has taken place? And "foster a love of neighbor" most likely refers to something the teacher sets out to do. In the terminology of Chapter Two, these are goal statements and they provide virtually no help in following the decision-making flow in an output model: articulate learning, design assessments to match, teach to achievement.

If we state the learning as "to become aware of computer applications in math," what assessment do we use for students to demonstrate the learning? A teacher could give them a multiple choice test asking them to correctly identify software programs and their uses. He could show a film on using computers for math applications in a variety of business settings and ask students to summarize the information or comment on computer use and effectiveness in these settings in a short paper. He could give them problems and/or projects that require the use of various computer applications.

Each of these possible assessments asks students to demonstrate *different* learning. Which is right? Which is more compatible with the mission, philosophy and integrative graduation outcomes of the school? The first assessment tests recall of information. The second assessment moves students to demonstrating comprehension and possibly doing some application and analysis, but still in the realm of manipulating ideas and information *about* computer applications. The third suggested assessment asks students to actually *use* computer applications in specific situations. Even here we might find a range of learning: Does the teacher specify which application to use in each situation, or is the determination of appropriate applications *by the student* part of the learning?

When we use goal statements to articulate curriculum, we have no basis beyond teacher preference, background, experience or habit on which to select appropriate assessments of learning and those strategies most likely to promote the intended learning. In some classrooms, this goal, "become aware of computer applications in math", will lead to recall of information alone; in other classrooms, the teacher will expect nothing short of proficient use of computer applications in a variety of real-life situations. What constitutes *significant* learning (as defined by the community values and subject-area experts) in relation to this subject matter for these students? As professional educators, we owe it to our students to ask this question and answer it in a way that will give direction to *all* educators teaching this part of the curriculum. In this way, we can assure some equity in learning across classes.

Consider the following statements which transform the goals listed at the beginning of this chapter into outcomes:

- To use a computer for problem-solving

- To explain the placement of elements in the periodic table.

- To integrate appropriate references to Shakespeare into conversation and written work.

- To design a multimedia presentation on some aspect of Mexican life and culture.

- To create and demonstrate situations which show love of neighbor.

- To research and present a current interpretation of one of the first ten amendments.

Each of these statements meets the two requirements of a student learning outcome: 1) stated from the student's point of view and 2) indicating observable behavior. As the basis for articulating a curriculum, these statements provide clear direction for decision-making.

In effect, each of these outcomes relates what constitutes significant learning of the subject matter for these students in this period of instruction in this school. If students can use a computer for problem-solving, they have achieved the important learning regarding computer applications in math. If students can integrate appropriate references to Shakespeare into conversation and written work, they are demonstrating important affective learning about Shakespeare. Significant learning about the Bill of Rights means being able to research and present a current interpretation of the first ten amendments.

Because these outcomes are clear statements of student learning, we can use them to follow the decision-making flow in an output model. Given the outcome (the statement of learning), "create and demonstrate situations which show love of neighbor," what assessment will we use to determine student learning? We could ask students to create and role play situations which show love of neighbor. We could ask students to write a case situation and decide what they would do if they were acting out of love of neighbor. We could ask students to observe and describe actions by fellow students in school that show love of neighbor. Although these suggestions identify different concrete assessments, each represents a valid indication of the desired learning stated in the outcome. That is, in doing any of these assessments well, students in fact "create and demonstrate situations which show love of neighbor".

To teach students in such a way that they will be able to do any of these assessments, a teacher would select strategies/activities/materials that help children connect the concept of love of neighbor and its Gospel roots with their own experiences. The stated outcome gives teachers direction for designing appropriate assessment tools and then selecting those teaching strategies/learning activities most likely to facilitate the learning. The fact that the observable learning identified in this outcome is "create and demonstrate" rather than "describe" or "name" situations that show love of neighbor, results from the process by which the school, in writing curriculum based on outcomes, has identified significant learning, not just any learning in relation to the subject matter.

If, instead, we begin with the goal statement "foster a love of neighbor," we would have no such clear direction for designing appropriate assessments and teaching strategies. What constitutes successful learning in relation to this goal? Since the statement is made from the teacher's point of view, we might focus on her behavior (input) and never even look for indications in the students that the intended learning is happening. If we do look to student behavior, what are we looking for? Definitions? Verbal responses prompted by worksheets? Actions? Goals may point us in a broad direction, but they do not focus upon the decision-making process enough to be real catalysts for increased learning and more dynamic teaching. Creating a curriculum based on goals will fall short of creating a curriculum that works.

Figures 4.1 and **4.2** offer some practice in differentiating goals and outcomes. Consider items (a) through (i) in **Figure 4.1**. Items b, d, e, and h are outcomes because they state what students will *do*. The other items are goals. We cannot observe a student understanding the principles of warm air. The student must *do* something that we will take as evidence that he in fact understands. Likewise for "appreciate" (f), "be aware of" (g) and "really understand" (i).

"Know how to" (item c) illustrates a goal statement that warrants special attention. At face value, we may all assume that "know how to add two digit numbers" means students will add two digit numbers. Not necessarily.

It could mean students will watch the teacher add and then explain what to do. In the simple case of two digit addition, this is quite unlikely. "Knowing how to add" probably does mean adding. But the statement is imprecise and will get us into trouble down the road.

Suppose the statement was "know how to perform the Heimlich maneuver." I know how to perform the Heimlich maneuver; that is, I can give you a clear and complete description of what do to. I have never performed the Heimlich maneuver on anyone who is choking, so perhaps I do not know how to perform the Heimlich maneuver in the only way that really counts.

If the intended learning is "add two digit numbers," it is clearer to simply state it than to leave room for misinterpretation by using phrases like "know how to" and "learn to."

The second two sets of examples in **Figure 4.1** illustrate the same point. In the first set, item (b) is the outcome. This is what students will *do* if they have achieved significant learning about these two French sounds. One might say that "will be able to pronounce" is precisely what "will have a good understanding of" and "will know the difference between" means. However, I have been in enough language classrooms to affirm that "understanding" and "knowing the difference" might well mean understanding the teacher's spoken word rather than producing it well oneself.

Without a clear student learning outcome about oral proficiency, teachers have no clear need for oral assessments. And in the absence of oral assessments, teaching strategies/learning activities need not focus on the students' spoken words. On the other hand, if the curriculum for French includes this outcome, valid assessment must include oral performance and teaching strategies/learning activities designed to coach oral proficiency must be part of the instructional process. Stating the curriculum in terms of learning outcomes gives us a clear basis for making the full range of decisions that are part of every conscious teaching/learning interaction. Significant outcomes, those that are central to the subject matter and useful beyond school, move us in the direction of more dynamic, student-centered teaching and assessment.

Item (b) in the second set of statements on the bottom of **Figure 4.1**. states what students will do to demonstrate significant learning about punctuation. They will "use correct punctuation in written work." On the basis of this outcome statement, the teacher can design valid assessments and select appropriate teaching/learning strategies to facilitate the stated learning.

Figure 4.1

Differentiating Goals and Outcomes

Goal: A statement of broad direction, general purpose or intent; vague; involves non–observable behavior.

Learning Outcome: A clear statement of what the learner is to do to demonstrate learning at the end of a period of instruction; involves observable behavior.

Observing Behavior: Behavior is acting—a way of doing something. In order to know whether expected learning has occurred, a teacher must be able to see something happen.

Mark those statements that seem like goals with a "G"; those that seem like outcomes with an "O."

a. To understand the principles of warm air.

b. To write three examples of fear expressed by the character.

c. To know how to add two digit numbers.

d. To name the bones of the body.

e. To diagram the steps of the argument.

f. To appreciate the plays of Shakespeare.

g. To be aware of Jesus' love for us.

h. To defend your appraisal of *Romeo and Juliet* as a great love story.

i. To really understand the three branches of government.

Here are three statements for a French class. Which one is in outcomes language?

a. The student will have a good understanding of the difference between the "*e*" sound in "*en*" and "*et*."

b. The student will be able to pronounce the French sounds "*en*" and "*et*" correctly.

c. The student will know the difference between the "*e*" sound in "*en*" and "*et*."

Which one is in outcomes language?

a. The student will have an adequate comprehension of the mechanics of punctuation.

b. The student will use correct punctuation in written work.

Part I : a.G, b.O, c.G, d.O, e.O, f.G, g.G, h.O, i.G.

Part II : b and b.

Figure 4.2

Goal or Outcome/Objective?

Write G in the space if the statement is a goal or write O if the statement is an outcome/objective.

1. To draw a picture of your best friend. _____
2. To analyze a work of literature for theme and form. _____
3. To help students improve sibling relationships. _____
4. To familiarize the student with reading and making graphs. _____
5. To express musical knowledge by composing. _____
6. To simplify algebraic expressions using the distributive property. _____
7. To develop a positive attitude toward math. _____
8. To recite bits of poetry. _____
9. To integrate current issues and events into classroom discussion. _____
10. To create a graphic design using a *Logo*. _____
11. To carry on intelligible conversation in Spanish using vocabulary and language structures presented in class. _____
12. To discuss three ways we can imitate the Good Shepherd. _____
13. To solve word problems requiring single digit multiplication. _____
14. To give examples of things you do at home and at school to keep healthy. _____
15. To become aware of computer applications in math and language arts. _____
16. To write a unified composition of 3-5 paragraphs on a single topic. _____
17. To understand the history and structure of the Catholic Church. _____
18. To critique a novel in an essay or oral report. _____
19. To effectively use a variety of research sources in the completion of a quarter project. _____
20. To compare and contrast the characteristics of acids, bases and salts. _____
21. To appreciate that music is as varied as the people who compose and perform it. _____
22. To study Spanish-speaking cultures. _____
23. To formulate a specific forecast based on observations, measurements, and relationships between variables. _____
24. To share a personal prayer experience. _____
25. To know how to follow directions. _____

(Key: 1.O, 2.O, 3.G, 4.G, 5.O, 6.O, 7.G, 8.O, 9.O, 10.O, 11.O, 12.O, 13.O, 14.O, 15.G, 16.O, 17.G, 18.O, 19.O 20.O, 21.G, 22.G, 23.O, 24.O, 25.G)

A valid assessment would involve correct punctuation in the students' written work. An objective, multiple choice, matching test alone would *not* be a true indication of the stated learning. Teaching strategies and learning activities needed to promote correct punctuation in written work would necessarily include many opportunities for students to write and receive feedback and coaching about punctuation in their writing. A teacher might use worksheets and objective tests as skill drills on specific aspects of correct punctuation, but these could not stand alone given the stated learning outcome. However, if item (a) were the statement of intended learning in the curriculum, drill and practice activities followed by an objective test could constitute all of the teaching/learning interactions on this subject matter.

More and more research confirms that learning discrete skills in isolation from the real world contexts in which the skills must be used does not result in competent performance. Completing drill and practice worksheets on correct punctuation does not necessarily—or even probably—lead to using correct punctuation in written work. To transfer correct punctuation skills to writing, students must practice those skills in writing and receive teacher feedback and coaching in that context. Stating curriculum in terms of learning outcomes gives us tremendous power to identify those multifaceted performances that constitute significant learning for our students. Once identified, they serve as the basis for the rest of our curriculum decision-making.

Figure 4.2 lists twenty-five statements taken from elementary and secondary curriculum guides and course syllabi. All of them were called "outcomes" or "objectives" in the documents in which they appeared. In terms of the distinctions made in Chapter Two, some are actually goal statements. **The first important step in designing and implementing an outcomes-centered curriculum consists in clearly differentiating goals and outcomes/objectives.** The more comfortable teachers and administrators become about recognizing outcomes and goals and then about transforming goals into outcomes, the easier the curriculum development process becomes.

Take a minute to do the exercise in **Figure 4.2** In most cases, the key to recognizing an outcome lies with the an active voice verb and an observable behavior. Since we are interested in student learning outcomes, the verb specifies what *students* will do. Some of these statements are more specific than others; some are more concrete and represent smaller periods of instruction. Earlier books on behavioral objectives often identified four essential parts to an objective: the **learning** (what is to be learned), the **behav-**

ior (what the student will do to demonstrate he has mastered the learning), the **performance level** (how well the behavior must be done), and the **conditions** (the parameters within which the behavior is to take place). In writing outcomes as the articulation of significant learning in the curriculum, the first two elements are essential. A student learning outcome must indicate the learning and the behavior, what is to be learned (subject matter) and what the student is expected to be able to do in relation to the subject matter.

Some outcomes will also include performance level and possibly parameters, but these latter two characteristics may more precisely appear in the sample assessments and criteria for evaluation. In other words, **the outcomes themselves will not specify everything a teacher needs to effectively coach students to mastery.** The outcomes themselves will set broad parameters within which teachers make other instructional decisions. By specifying what students who have achieved the intended learning will do, we take the first step in a decision-making process that then specifies the expected level of performance and the teaching/learning conditions required to bring it about.

When determining whether a statement is an outcome or a goal, it helps to ask the question: Does this statement give me a clear idea about what I would ask students to do to show the learning? If, after reading the statement, I still find myself saying, "O.K., but what will I take as evidence that this has occurred?", the statement is a goal. For example, the goal statement "to understand the history and structure of the Catholic Church" (Item 17 in **Figure 4.2**) does not give a clear picture of what students will do to show the learning. I still have to ask, "What will I take as evidence that students 'understand?' Will they explain the history of the church, orally or in writing? Will they give examples of how the history and structure of the church have influenced current practice in some area? Will they evaluate the church's social teachings from a historical perspective?" They might do any one of these, but each represents different levels of learning and requires students to demonstrate different degrees of complexity in interacting with the subject matter. A curriculum that works avoids this kind of ambiguity.

Item 2 in Figure 4.2 often causes differences of opinion among faculties with which I have used this exercise. Some see this statement as a goal because "we can't see students 'analyze'." In my opinion, what makes this statement an outcome comes from the fact that it describes a *specific* and identifiable cognitive response on the part of students. If I asked students to analyze *Where the Red Fern Grows* for theme and form, and they gave me a summary of the plot or a description of the setting and mood, I would clearly know that they had not demonstrated the stated learning. Again, to be an outcome, a statement must indicate what *students* will *do* clearly enough that we will agree about what to look for if the learning has been achieved.

An outcome need not necessarily spell out performance level or other relevant conditions. The crucial point (and the reason I do not insist on including all four elements in every outcome statement) is to view outcomes as pivotal statements of observable student learning, not as all-inclusive, absolutely precise scope and sequence indicators. In the former capacity, outcomes give us tremendous power to engage in curriculum decision-making aimed at increasing significant learning for all our students; outcomes in these terms are freeing and generative. When we become overly concerned with specifying details in each outcome regardless of the level, we run the risk of succumbing to the down side of behavioral objectives, namely, a kind of behaviorism that reduces learning to a checklist of seemingly discrete skills.

In **Figure 4.2.**, goal statements 3 and 4 are written from the teachers' point of view. **We must state learning outcomes from the student's point of view.** Item 24 presents an affective outcome. It qualifies as an outcome because it states what students will do to demonstrate learning. In this case, students will "share a personal prayer experience." The statement tells us what to look for; it is clear enough that we would be able to agree about whether it happened. If a student recounted someone else's prayer experience or simply did not present a prayer experience of her own in any form, we would know the outcome had not been achieved.

Figures 4.3 and **4.4** provide additional practice in differentiating goals and outcomes. As in **Figure 4.2**, the outcomes in these exercises represent different levels of specificity and different scopes of instruction. All the items labeled *outcomes* have two things in common: stated from the student's point of view and indicating observable behavior. In **Figure 4.3**, goal statements 6 and 17 are stated from the teacher's point of view. Items 4 and 8 are affective outcomes. In **Figure 4.4**, goal statements 1 and 8 are stated from the teacher's point of view. Outcomes 3, 7, 11 and 13 indicate affective learning.

Three items in **Figure 4.4** require additional comment.

Although the key identifies item 2 as an outcome, it is very poorly stated. To say the students will "develop the ability to write a character sketch" almost certainly means the students will be able to write a character sketch. But in the way it is stated originally, the emphasis falls on the noun (*ability*) rather than on the verb (*write*), resulting in a much less dynamic statement of intended learning. "Write a character sketch" makes a much clearer statement.

Figure 4.3

Goal or Outcome/Objective?

Write G in the space if the statement is a goal or write O if the statement is an outcome/objective.

1. To evaluate the contribution of significant men and women in world history _____
2. To understand the roles played by racial and ethnic groups in American society. _____
3. To name the key events of Jesus' life and to explain central themes of the gospels. _____
4. To quote a scripture passage that reflects a moral principle you act on. _____
5. To use the writing/revision process in the writing of essays. _____
6. To strengthen student research skills. _____
7. To develop confidence in their ability to communicate through music. _____
8. To use taste and smell words to describe your room. _____
9. To develop a respect and appreciation for people of other cultures._____
10. To explore our human understanding and experience of Jesus. _____
11. To state their own beliefs about Jesus in a short paper. _____
12. To ask significant questions. _____
13. To apply the language and techniques of Algebra to the solution of real world problems. _____
14. To collect objects from nature that show the change of seasons. _____
15. To learn basic principles of tumbling. _____
16. To construct an accurate flow chart for an original program. _____
17. To instill a love for reading. _____
18. To use value and perspective in a two-dimensional charcoal sketch. _____

(Key: 1.O, 2.G, 3.O, 4.O, 5.O, 6.G, 7.G, 8.O, 9.G, 10.G, 11.O, 12.O, 13.O, 14.O, 15.G, 16.O, 17.G, 18.O)

Likewise, items 3 and 11 are technically outcomes because they do indicate, broadly speaking, what students will do. So long as we agree on what cooperativeness looks like, outcome 3 tells us students will do this. So long

---

Figure 4.4

Goal or Outcome/Objective?

Write G in the space if the statement is a goal or write O if the statement is an outcome/objective.

1.   Deepen students' understanding of Christian morality as responsibility for the welfare of others.   _____

2.   Develop the ability to write a character sketch.   _____

3.   Demonstrate cooperativeness in working with others.   _____

4.   Determine the main idea and sequence when it is not explicitly stated.   _____

5.   Trace scriptural origins of the contemporary church's celebrations.   _____

6.   Discuss communication and adjustment within marriage and family.   _____

7.   Express empathy toward victims of social injustice and prejudice.   _____

8.   Lead the students to see the communal dimension of morality.   _____

9.   Engage in free conversation in Spanish within the limits of the material.   _____

10.   Use precise language in definitions and explanations of scientific concepts.   _____

11.   Demonstrate a positive attitude toward physical activity as a preferred use of leisure time.   _____

12.   Organize and generalize from data collected in experiments.   _____

13.   Independently initiate learning.   _____

14.   Become more informed about the implications of technology in her present and future life.   _____

15.   Make sound decisions based on sufficient reflection and knowledge.   _____

16.   Learn basic historical concepts such as democracy, feudalism, socialism, communism, colonialism, and nationalism.   _____

(Key: 1.G, 2.O, 3.O, 4.O, 5.O, 6.O, 7.O, 8.G, 9.O, 10.O, 11.O, 12.O, 13.O,14.G, 15.O, 16.G)

as we all recognize a positive attitude toward physical activity as a preferred use of leisure time, outcome 11 tells us to look for students showing that attitude. These two statements are from the student's point of view and indicate observable behavior, but only in very broad terms. They would best function at the level of graduation or subject area outcomes. As course or grade level outcomes, they would be weak.

Once a faculty feels comfortable differentiating goals and outcomes/objectives, teachers might work together to practice transforming goals into outcomes. For example, returning to **Figure 4.2**, we might transform Goal 4 into the following outcome: "Students will make and read graphs." To be more specific: "Students will present data in bar, line and circle graphs and read the graphs correctly." Either statement tells us what students will do to demonstrate learning and either one gives us a basis for continuing the curriculum decision-making flow.

Here are a few more sample transformations from **Figure 4.2**. Item 7, "to develop a positive attitude toward math," can be transformed into "to speak positively about his ability to do math"; "to express positive body language while in math class"; "to volunteer examples of the usefulness of math"; or "to choose additional math classes." Item 15, "to become aware of computer applications in language arts," can be transformed into: "to use Word Perfect 6.0, Spell Check and Writer's Workbench in writing papers," or, less specifically, "to use word processing software in writing papers"; or "to describe software programs available to assist in writing."

The last set of examples brings us to another important aspect of writing outcomes. First, be sure the statements are truly outcomes rather than goals. Secondly, examine what's inside the outcomes.

Since an outcome must contain two elements, the *content* of the learning and the *doing* in relation to the content, we can think of outcomes as placing learning on the learning grid represented in **Figure 4.5**. The vertical axis represents level of difficulty of the subject matter. For example, in terms of difficulty we might order subject matter in language arts as follows: sentence, paragraph, one-page essay, short story, novel. Or we might order subject matter in mathematics in terms of difficulty: whole numbers, fractions, single variable equations, linear functions, infinities. Or we might order subject matter in basketball in terms of difficulty: passing the ball, dribbling, free throws, outside shooting, playing an effective game as center, full court press. Traditional scope and sequence charts pay a lot of attention to ordering learning in terms of perceived level of difficulty of subject matter. But this tells only half the story.

Consider **Figure 4.6**. For each subject matter illustrated, there are six different student responses to the subject matter, six different things students could do to indicate learning. The example presents six responses in ascending order of complexity of thinking.

If a school's curriculum guide identifies the short story as a topic for learning or expresses the goal "students will learn about the short story" or "increase their understanding of the short story," what does this tell us? In terms of level of difficulty, it tells us that students are learning beyond the level of sentences and paragraphs. It tells us nothing about what they will do to demonstrate significant learning about the subject matter. The six outcome statements in each sample do define the learning—in six different ways. Each of the six statements, as a statement of what is to be learned, would lead to different assessment tools to allow students to show learning and to different teaching/learning strategies to promote the stated learning.

In a class where the point of studying the short story is to define elements in your own words and to illustrate those elements in specific stories, the emphasis could well be on teacher talk and written tests. In a class where the intended learning of studying the short story is to write a story focusing on a particular element or to critique stories based on developed criteria, the emphasis must be on more active learning and higher order thinking. Which outcome actually defines the curriculum will depend on the broader, integrative learning outcomes expressed in mission, philosophy, and graduation outcomes.

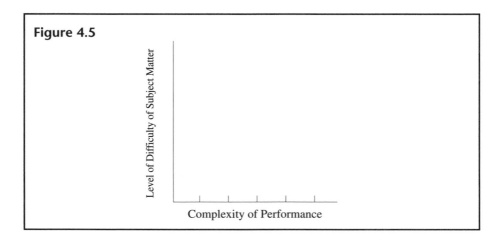

Figure 4.5

Level of Difficulty of Subject Matter

Complexity of Performance

The same remains true for the subject matter *full court press*. Stating curriculum in terms of "understanding full court press" or "learning about full court press" identifies only the subject matter, not the student's expected response to that subject matter. Without both pieces, we have no clear basis for the full range of curriculum decision-making; we have no basis for designing valid assessments and selecting appropriate teaching strategies/ learning activities to bring about the stated learning.

Learning is not subject matter or content alone; learning is *responding* to the subject matter or content. Stating curriculum in terms of learning outcomes requires us to locate the desired learning on both axes of the learning grid illustrated in **Figure 4.5**. Without both pieces we waste time and resources and cut ourselves off from an important tool with which to evaluate the quality and equity of our instructional programs.

Research and experience continue to confirm that *all* students learn better when they are presented with a rich curriculum that expects higher order thinking and allows more active learning. Honors courses that treat vast amounts of difficult material almost completely on the level of recalling information on tests do an equal disservice to students as lower level courses that remain fixed on drill and practice of isolated skills. Reserving simulations, non-routine problem-solving and team learning for upper level students puts limits on learning for others.

Figure 4.6

Short Story

1. Name the elements of a short story.
2. Give definitions in own words.
3. Illustrate the theme of this story.
4. Compare the theme of this story with the theme of another story by the same author.
5. Write a short story using this theme.
6. Critique the story using criteria developed in class.

Full Court Press

1. State the rules of basketball relating to use of full court press.
2. Explain full court press strategy.
3. Use full court press in practice scrimmage.
4. Analyze video for personal errors in executing full court press.
5. Design game plan for use of full court press.
6. Critique team performance.

In an input model of curriculum development, many such limits to learning go unheeded because the focus stays on the content and the teacher's sense of what to do with it. Often, unexamined practices shape teaching decisions. I may assume that I teach for higher thinking (perhaps my goals state that I do), but, in practice, 90% of my tests ask for recall of information. Commitment to stating curriculum in terms of learning outcomes gives us a powerful tool to examine the match (or lack of one) between what we *say* we want students to learn, what we *use* to see if they have learned, and the *methods* we use to help them learn. Chapter six addresses this match in greater detail.

Stating curriculum in terms of outcomes gives us a common language to talk about student learning across the curriculum and within pieces of the curriculum. It gives us a way of reviewing whether what we have identified as significant learning (the stated outcomes), when taken as a whole, really represents the significant learning we intended. For example, if we accurately articulate the outcomes for middle school science and we find that they all say "list", "explain", "state", "name", "define", "give examples", it becomes fairly clear that the teaching focuses on transmission of information even if the curriculum outline talks about the impact of science on life and the importance of hands-on learning.

Figure 4.7 presents a short summary of Bloom's taxonomy of cognitive skills. This cognitive taxonomy, like the affective and psychomotor taxonomies, provides a useful way of screening outcomes for level of complexity of response to subject matter. (The materials in this book use the order of skills in Bloom's original taxonomy; Bloom later reversed synthesis and evaluation. Both represent higher order, divergent thinking and the exact placement is not significant for our purposes.)

Figure 4.8 gives examples of outcomes/objectives for each level of Bloom's taxonomy, using three different subject matters: World War I, math problem solving, and reading. **Figure 4.9** provides additional examples of the progression represented in the taxonomy from the point of view of *questions* teachers ask. **Figure 4.10** presents a simplified outline of the cognitive, affective and psychomotor taxonomies for reference. Using the taxonomies to review outcomes provides one useful tool for going beyond the initial question, "Are these truly outcomes?", to the second question, "Do they represent significant learning?" That is, does the learning stated in the outcomes for grade levels/clusters and courses represent learning that is central to the subject matter, useful beyond the classroom, and connected to community values?

Figure 4.7

Using Bloom's Taxonomy In Writing Outcomes

Taxonomy	Identifying Characteristics	Verbs		
1. **Knowledge**	Eliciting factual answers, testing recall and recognition; recall	define label list name	recall recite record repeat	select point out reproduce memorize
2. **Comprehension**	Translating, interpreting, extrapolating; putting information in own words	describe discuss explain identify indicate	outline recognize restate select	translate match tell summarize
3. **Application**	Use of information or skill, application to situations that are new, unfamiliar, or have a new slant for students Minimum level we have to teach to so as not to have wasted our time.	apply construct explain select	identify illustrate interpret dramatize	demonstrate show how employ
4. **Analysis**	Breaking down into parts; relating parts to the whole *"Higher Order"* thinking begins with analysis.	analyze arrange chart compare distinguish	diagram dissect criticize examine	debate relate contrast plan
5. **Synthesis**	Combining elements into a pattern not clearly there before; involve divergent thinking and many possible answers. Where there is more than one correct answer "What if ...?"	arrange write construct create design develop	formulate make plan prepare propose solve	compose forecast estimate tell do
6. **Evaluation**	Judge according to some set of criteria, and state why.	appraise assess defend criticize	dispute evaluate grade choose	verify decide judge why

Henry Hammer, FMS

Figure 4.8

Bloom's Taxonomy:
Examples of Outcomes/Objectives on Each Level

Knowledge:

List the causes of World War I.

Recall the steps for solving this equation.

Name the characters in this story.

Comprehension:

Give an example of economic instability at the time that led to World War I.

Explain how you would solve this kind of problem.

Describe what each character did in the story.

Application:

Give a present day example of the kind of economic
instability that led to World War I.

Solve this equation.

Tell about any times your friends have been faced with the same problems as in the story.

Analysis:

Compare the causes of World War I and the Bolshevik Revolution.

Analyze this problem and tell how to solve it.

Look at this story and tell what's missing from the list of important elements.

Synthesis:

Build a scenario dealing with economic instability that would not lead to war.

Create three problems requiring this process for solving equations.

Rewrite the ending based on a different choice made by Susan.

Evaluation:

Evaluate the President's decision to declare war.

Appraise the clarity and breadth of the sample problems.

Rate this story and give reasons for your rating.

Figure 4.9

Question Classification According to Bloom's Taxonomy

I. Knowledge

Identifying Characteristics

1. Only recall or recognition of information from past experience, or from teacher presentation, from reading, etc., is required.
2. Little or possibly no understanding of the information is required.
3. The learner is not asked to compare, relate, or make any inductive or deductive leap on his/her own.

Examples

1. What were the names of Columbus' ships?
2. What are the main functions of the circulatory system?
3. Who are the characters in the story?
4. What are the rules for volleyball?
5. How many inches are there in a yard?

Verbs to use in question formation

repeat   recite   recall   define   record   name   list

II. Comprehension

Identifying Characteristics

1. The emphasis is on change of form.
2. Some extension beyond what is given in the original may be required.
3. Relationships are stressed.
4. The learner goes beyond recall or rote memorization to meaning.

Examples

1. What information can we get from this map?
2. What concept does this cartoon illustrate?
3. How would you describe the mood created in this poem?
4. Explain your answer for this multiplication problem.
5. Why should we stand up straight when singing?
6. Restate the definition of zero-based budgeting in your own words.
7. What are some examples of pollution shown in the film?

Verbs to use in question formation

restate   recognize   identify   discuss   explain   describe

III.   Application

Identifying Characteristics

1. Deals with usable knowledge and emphasizes *use* of information or skill.
2. The whole of ideas and skills are dealt with rather than just the parts.
3. Contains a minimum of directions or instructions because the questions are based on previous learning and the student is expected to know what to do. He/she selects what information is appropriate for use in the new situation.

Examples

1. Show us how to say "Hello. How are you?" in sign language.
2. Use long division to solve this problem.
3. How does this gospel story relate to your own life?

continued on next page

Figure 4.9 continued

4. What punctuation marks belong in this paragraph?
5. To what extent does this novel illustrate the theme of human against nature?
6. Using the directional words we've learned, how would you give someone directions to go from our classroom to the lunchroom?
7. Use a ruler to measure your desk.
8. What are some examples of democracy we see in our school?
9. How do civil rights apply to excluding students with AIDS from school?

Verbs

use	show	interpret	apply	demonstrate	illustrate

IV. Analysis

Identifying Characteristics

1. Student uses/builds knowledge of rules of reasoning. (Working with this level question provides practice in using reasoning skills.)
2. Question deals with both form and content.
3. Process begins by breaking a communication or problem into constituent parts (premise, assumption , hypothesis, supporting data, conclusions, etc.).

Examples

1. How do these two stories differ?
2. Why did a city grow in this place?
3. How can we test this hypothesis?
4. How would you solve this problem?
5. What is the same about these two pictures?
6. How could you make this sentence more interesting?
7. After reading these Gospel stories, make five statements you think are true about Jesus.
8. Listen to what I say and tell me what's wrong.
9. What is the difference between $3x+4$ and $3(x+4)$?

Verbs

distinguish	contrast	compare	debate	analyze
examine	criticize	relate	infer	conclude

V. Synthesis

Identifying Characteristics

1. Emphasis on creation of an original product (combining parts of past experience to create a new whole).
2. Involves divergent thinking and many possible answers.

Examples

1. On the basis of our study of the problems of a city, what solution to the transportation problem would you propose?
2. What game strategy would you formulate for the next eighth grade girls' basketball game?
3. Write your own poem about snow.
4. What are three questions about this story we could ask that begin, "What if. . ."?
5. Make a puppet that shows one of the feelings we've been talking about.
6. Make up three problems that use multiplication.
7. Create an ad for a product you create.
8. Plan a CCD class for fourth graders on reconciliation.
9. What is the common theme in all these stories?

continued on next page

Figure 4.9 continued

10. What hypothesis would best explain this data?

Verbs

adapt   compose   create   formulate   generate   imagine   invent

VI. Evaluation

Identifying Characteristics

1. Emphasis on judgment.
2. Only those evaluations that are or can be made with distinct criteria in mind are considered. It is not merely an opinion based on a snap decision.
3. Involves assessment.

Examples

1. Do you think that the *Eighteenth Amendment* is a good law?
2. Which of the two children in the story is more helpful? Give reasons for your answer.
3. Is this a good adventure story? Give reasons for your answer.
4. Assess the reasons given by the citizens for the *Boston Tea Party*. Were they valid or not? On what basis?
5. If we believe in Jesus, do we have to give money to poor people who ask us?
6. Evaluate this painting.

Verbs

appraise   assess   conclude   judge   measure   decide   defend   rate

Figure 4.10

Learning Skills
Cognitive, Affective, and Psycho–Motor Behaviors to Be Developed in the Students
Cognitive Skills

I. Knowledge

Ability to gather information.
Ability to recall facts, principles, generalizations, formulas.
Ability to memorize important data.
Example: To list the five main parts of a 35mm camera.

2. Comprehension

Ability to understand important facts and principles.
Ability to report the results of study.
Ability to explain or interpret data in student's own words.
Example: To describe the sequence of six steps for loading film into a 35mm camera.

3. Application

Ability to apply principles to student's own life and experience.

continued on next page

Figure 4.10 continued

Ability to use rules, laws, concepts generalizations in a new problem situation.

Ability to use guides and dependable sources of information for solving everyday problems.

Ability to apply known solutions to new events.

Ability to apply new skills to solve problems.

Example: To choose the camera exposure settings for various picture–taking situations.

4. Analysis

Ability to think clearly and analytically.

Ability to compare and contrast.

Ability to show a relationship between parts of a whole.

Ability to take apart elements of an object or event for more careful study.

Ability to use logical reasoning in problem solving.

Example: To determine the relationship of exposure settings and lens type to the finished photographs.

5. Synthesis

Ability to create a unique response to a problem or situation.

Ability to produce a new plan of operation.

Ability to contribute new ways of viewing well–worn solutions.

Ability to draw generalizations from a collection of specific facts or items of data.

Ability to express oneself creatively in a particular field of endeavor.

Ability to communicate clearly one's own ideas, feelings, questions.

Example: To plan a series of six subjects for a photographic slide sequence.

6. Evaluation

Ability to formulate an opinion based on relevant data.

Ability to judge the worth of an object or event based on internal or external criteria.

Ability to support a position following careful analysis of the situation.

Example: To rate the quality of slides on a 4 point scale.

Affective Skills

1.   Receiving

Willingness to listen attentively.

Willingness to observe a situation or event in such a way as to become aware of it.

Example: Student listens to an announcement about a meeting to organize a new ecology club.

2.   Responding

Willingness to perform a task.

Willingness to volunteer for a job or activity.

Willingness to answer a question.

Willingness to develop interests.

Willingness to develop sensitivities.

Example: Student attends the first ecology club meeting.

continued on next page

Figure 4.10 continued

3.   Valuing

Willingness to express a preference.

Willingness to choose something on one's own.

Willingness to recruit others to one's own point of view.

Willingness to express appreciation for positive aspects of a situation, event, object, idea.

Willingness to respect another's point of view.

Example: At the meeting, the student votes for a resolution to have a student clean–up day.

4.   Organizing

Willingness to include a belief, idea, action, attitude into student's normal routine.

Willingness to change an opinion or alter a belief on the basis of chosen values.

Willingness to stick to a position.

Ability to incorporate a belief, idea, action, attitude into student's own value system.

Example: Student decides to attend a second club meeting rather than going to a ball game.

5.   Characterizing

Ability to behave in a predictable manner.

Ability to develop a lifestyle consistent with chosen values.

Ability to live by a philosophy.

Ability to relate well to others.

Example: Student continues an active participation in the club over a period of years.

Psycho–Motor Skills

1. Imitation

Ability to mimic actions requiring low levels of coordination.

Example: Pick up blocks.

2. Manipulation

Ability to follow directions in handling or moving objects with actions requiring low levels of coordination.

Example: Stack blocks in simple patterns.

3. Precision

Ability to imitate and manipulate with a degree of accuracy, exactness and control.

Example: Build complete structure with blocks.

4. Articulation

Ability to coordinate a series of actions requiring accuracy as well as speed.

Example: Use blocks to build a complicated structure according to a specified design in a given time frame.

5. Naturalization

Ability to articulate in automatic and spontaneous ways. An action is routine, natural and smooth.

Example: Create alternative structure easily and quickly in response to a design problem.

Figure 4.11 offers additional input on and examples of affective outcomes/objectives. Some educators shy away from using outcomes as the basis for curriculum decision-making on the assumption that only easily measured cognitive learning can be articulated in outcomes language. One of the operating premises of this approach to curriculum development is that we can articulate any learning we are after in outcomes terms. Further, disciplining ourselves as professional educators to do this will help us eliminate wishful-thinking curriculum and strengthen higher achieving curriculum.

Significant learning must include affective learning. When we can comfortably and accurately articulate affective learning in outcomes language, we gain the same power in instructional decision-making and delivery that we do in articulating cognitive outcomes. Affective outcomes define the significant learning in terms of what *students* will *do* in the affective domain in relation to the subject matter. Once the learning is defined, the outcomes serve as the basis for answering the other questions in the decision-making flow: what assessments will we use to let students demonstrate the learning? What strategies will best facilitate performance? **Figure 4.12** presents two additional sets of affective outcomes/objectives following the complexity progression in the affective taxonomy.

Becoming more conscious of affective learning outcomes allows us to be more conscious about *combining* cognitive and affective learning in outcomes that articulate richer, more complex, more significant learning. **Figure 4.13** presents a few examples of cognitive/affective combination outcomes. **Figure 4.14** offers parallel ways of indicating learning behavior at the various levels of the affective and cognitive domains.

Levels of Outcomes

A student learning outcome is a statement of what students will do to indicate learning as a result of instruction. The period of instruction ranges from the entire educational program of a school (graduation outcomes) to a single lesson (lesson objectives). Outcomes-centered curriculum for elementary schools would include graduation outcomes, K-8 subject area outcomes, grade level/cluster outcomes, and unit outcomes; for secondary schools, curriculum would include graduation outcomes, program level outcomes (department/division outcomes), course outcomes, and unit outcomes. **Lesson objectives belong in the lesson plans of individual teachers, not in the written curriculum of the school.**

Figures 4.15 and 4.16 provide examples of elementary and secondary outcomes at each of the four levels. In a well designed, well aligned curriculum, connections among outcomes at each level will be apparent to teachers and administrators, and can be communicated to students and parents. That is, unit outcomes are shaped by grade level/cluster or course outcomes; grade level/cluster and course outcomes are shaped by K-8 subject area or departmental outcomes; and these latter are shaped by graduation outcomes.

Graduation outcomes articulate the significant, rich and multidimensional, integrated learning by which the educational program is to be ultimately measured consistent with the philosophy and mission of the school. K-8 subject area and departmental outcomes focus the graduation outcomes in terms of broad subject matter and learning disciplines. Grade level/cluster and course outcomes tell us what students will do on their way toward achieving K-8 and departmental outcomes, toward graduation outcomes. Unit outcomes provide helpful benchmarks of student learning on the way to achieving grade level/cluster and course outcomes, and so on.

Figure 4.17 shows an example of elementary alignment apparent through articulation of outcomes from one level to the next. The top half of the page illustrates the process of articulating significant learning throughout the curriculum starting with a graduation outcome. If a school has as one of its graduation outcomes, "Students will find the information they need", how will K-8 science instruction contribute to achieving that outcome? One answer: Students will use current and historical scientific materials to research answers to laboratory questions. In sixth grade science class, this K-8 outcome connects to more specific subject matter and age-appropriate skills: Students will use supplementary science books in the school library to interpret and explain their laboratory data. Within the sixth grade science class, a unit on systems has an outcome that connects the grade level science outcome to the specific content of the unit.

When the school uses a graduation outcome to shape choices about instructional design at the grade/cluster level and unit level, the explanation of why the teacher uses certain strategies becomes very straightforward. In this example, one of the reasons why the unit outcome includes research from supplementary sources is because using supplementary sources at the unit level promotes the use of supplementary sources in science instruction at the grade level and K-8 level, which give students opportunities to develop and demonstrate the graduation outcome, "find the information they need".

Figure 4.11

Affective Learning Skills

I. Receiving

1. Student demonstrates willingness to listen attentively.
2. Student demonstrates willingness to observe a situation or event in such a way as to become aware of it.
3. Student shows openness to idea, experience, event, attitude.

Verbs: listen   watch   view   observe   experience

Sample Outcomes/Objectives:

1. Student will view the film "Platoon" prior to a discussion about the implications of modern war.
2. Student will listen critically to the State of the Union speech.
3. Student will listen attentively to a fellow student's critique of the painting.
4. Student will observe a demonstration of the effects of smoking on lungs.
5. Student will experience acceptance in a cooperative work group.

II. Responding

1. Student demonstrates willingness to perform a task, answer a question, engage in an activity.
2. Student volunteers for a job or activity.
3. Student shows willingness to develop interests or sensitivities.
4. Student is willing to engage without any particular commitment.

Verbs: participate, attend, respond, engage in, volunteer, express feelings toward, experiment, explore, try, show interest in

Sample Outcomes/Objectives:

1. Student will participate in a variety of prayer experiences.
2. Student will try out alternative problem solving techniques.
3. Student will experiment with a variety of media introducing 3–D shapes.
4. Student will engage in a Spanish conversation with a fellow classmate.
5. Student will explore three different music styles.
6. Student will express his/her feelings about the main character.

III. Valuing

1. Student is willing to express a preference.
2. Student will express appreciation for positive aspects of a situation, event, object, idea.
3. Student will choose something on his/her own.
4. Student will recruit others to his/her own point of view.
5. Student respects another's point of view.
6. At this level, the student begins willingly to act on personal value.

Verbs: choose, express a preference, show appreciation, show respect for, speak in favor of

Sample Outcomes/Objectives:

1. Student will choose a corporation to manage during the course.

continued on next page

Figure 4.11 continued

2. Student will express a preference for a particular style of music and give reasons for his/her preference.
3. Student will show appreciation for the aesthetic dimension of nature by willingly including comments about beauty, symmetry, and simplicity in scientific reports.
4. Student will use his/her own life experience to express the value of reconciliation and forgiveness.
5. Student will volunteer to use the computer for writing a research paper.
6. Student is able to express positive feelings about herself/himself as a math student.

IV. Organizing

1. Student begins to include a belief, idea, action, attitude into his/her normal routine.
2. Student will change an opinion or alter a belief on the basis of chosen values.
3. Student will stick to a position.
4. Student demonstrates the ability to incorporate a belief, idea, action, attitude into his/her own value system.
5. At this level, the student begins acting consistently and over time in relation to a value.

Verbs: continue to express, act on the basis of the value, interpret in light of the belief that, in light of the attitude that, in the light of valuing of

Sample Outcomes/Objectives:

1. Student will continue to practice the Catholic faith in the face of critiquing some Church practices.
2. Student will use his/her acceptance of the theory of evolution to explain the development of a species.
3. Student will interpret rightness of a decision on the basis of her/his stated values.
4. Student will show respect for fellow students in a wide variety of situations.
5. Student will continue physical fitness routines outside of class.
6. Student will read literature books for pleasure during summer.

V. Characterizing

1. Student behaves in a predictable manner.
2. Student develops a lifestyle consistent with chosen values.
3. Student lives by a philosophy.
4. Student relates well to others.
5. At this level, values clearly underlie commitment.

Verbs: continue over the long run, act consistently

Sample Outcomes/Objectives:

1. Student will make personal choices consistent with gospel values.
2. Student will act on the conviction that she/he can influence the well–being of the world.
3. Student will avoid substance abuse based on his/her convictions about healthy human behaviors.
4. Student will engage in personal reading throughout high school.

Figure 4.12

Sample Affective Outcomes/Objectives

Problem Solving

1. Student observes a variety of methods for solving a given kind of problem.
2. Student tries a method for solving the problem.
3. Student chooses a method for solving the problem.
4. Student favors one method over the others.
5. Whenever, she's faced with a certain kind of problem, she uses her preferred method to solve it.

Writing Style

1. Student reads prose writers with widely different styles.
2. Student writes small essays imitating the style of one or the other of the authors.
3. Student selects one style to use for his quarter essay.
4. Student adopts the style and begins using it regularly in his writing.
5. Student's authorship of a paper can be determined by its style.

Figure 4.13

Combining Cognitive/Affective Learning Skills

1. After exploring three different music styles, the student will state his/her preference and give reasons for the choice.
2. After exploring three different music styles, the student will evaluate each according to criteria developed in class.
3. After listening to students express their feelings about the main character, the student will write a character sketch including an assessment of the character's level of ethical development.
4. The student will identify values embedded in current consumerism and contrast these with gospel values. The student will explore the implications of each set of values and express a personal preference.
5. After experimenting with a variety of math manipulatives, the student will pick one and explain how he/she uses it to show equality.
6. The student will plan lunches for the week based on principles of good nutrition and choose to fix and eat them.
7. The student will design and participate in a scientific experiment on short–term memory.
8. The student will act collaboratively in problem solving.
9. The student will acknowledge at least one personal experience of acting on the call to transform the world.

Figure 4.14

Comparison of Cognitive and Affective Domain
(Levels by Bloom and Krathwohl)

This correlation appears in *Affective Direction: Planning and Teaching for Thinking and Feeling* by Eberle & Hall, 1987.

Level I:

Receiving:

To Attend To -

be alert	observe
be aware	pay attention
be conscious of	perceive
experience	scan
handle	see
hear	sense
heed	smell
listen	taste
look	touch
notice	watch

Knowledge:

To Know About-

cite	learn
color	list
copy	locate
diagram	name
draw	quote
find	recall
identify	recognize
itemize	remember
know about	repeat
label	spell

Level II:

Responding:

Willingness To Respond-

answer	follow
argue	gather
ask	offer
attempt	participate
comply	proceed
contribute	submit
cooperate	suggest
discuss	try
express	volunteer
find	interpret

Comprehension:

To Understand-

account for	outline
conclude	paraphrase
define	restate
demonstrate	retell
distinguish	reword
detail	show how
estimate	summarize
explain	tell about
illustrate	translate

Level III:

Valuing:

To Determine A Preference-

adopt	promote
advocate	propose
approve	rank
assign worth	rate
choose	recommend
decide	reject
defend	rely on
embrace	select

Application:

To Put To Use-

act on	operate
apply	paint
assemble	perform
construct	practice
dramatize	prepare
draw	produce
employ	put to use
exercise	role play

continued on next page

Figure 4.14 continued

honor	specify	form	sketch
pick	value	make	solve

Level IV:

Organization:	**Analysis:**	**Synthesis:**
To Establish A	To Break Into	Create-
Value System-	Parts-	
advocate	analyze	adapt
appraise	detect	alter
arrange	differentiate	compose
assess	discriminate	combine
co-ordinate	distinguish	create
classify	dissect	expand upon
compare	examine	formulate
design	explore	generalize
determine	intensify parts	generate
establish order	investigate	imagine
figure out	look into	improve
group	notice differences	integrate
organize	notice difficulties	invent
plan	notice methods	rearrange
propose	notice similarities	reorder
review	reason why	restate
scheme	sift out	revise
sort out	subdivide	rewrite
structure	unfold	reverse
systemize	unravel	synthesize

Level V:

Characterization:		**Evaluation:**	
To Live One's Beliefs-		To Judge For A Purpose-	
accept	do	apply standards	estimate
act on	proceed	appraise	evaluate
adopt	react	assess	judge
affirm	regulate	choose	measure
avoid	reject	compare	pronounce
behave	resist	conclude	rate
confide in	revise	contrast	rule on
declare	testify	decide	select
develop	transact	defend	test
disclose	trust	determine	value

Chart printed in *DYNAMITE in the Classroom: A How-To Handbook for Teachers*, Sandra L Schurr, National Middle School Association.

Figure 4.15   **Elementary School Outcomes**
                        (partial samples at various levels)

I. Upon graduation students should be able to:

- Read for information, meaning and enjoyment.
- Write clearly using proper sentence structure and proper spelling.
- Find the information they need.
- Practice good citizenship in school and the community.
- Use a computer for application.
- Form a judgment and give reasons.
- Express understanding of the relationship between God, self and others in attitudes of respect, understanding, caring and sharing.

II. K-8 Language Arts focuses instruction so that students will:

- Analyze and evaluate literature.
- Integrate information from various sources.
- Deliver message clearly and confidently.
- Use stages of writing process.
- Adjust listening strategies to fit the situation.

K-8 Religion focuses instruction so that students will:

- Express understanding of and appreciation for Christian revelation and tradition.
- Participate intelligently and respectfully in prayer and worship.
- Give service to the community.
- Relate Scripture to their own lives.

III. By the end of 8th grade/junior high language arts, students should be able to:

- Use different voice and presentation standards for different situations.
- Listen to make inferences and to raise questions.
- Show mood and imagery in writing through vocabulary and figurative language.
- Analyze the construction of simple paragraphs.

By the end of 5th grade/middle school religion, students will:

- State the seven sacraments and explain the importance of each.
- Plan and experience classroom liturgies.
- Demonstrate how the Works of Mercy can be incorporated into their daily lives.

IV. By the end of this unit, students will:

- Write a paragraph conveying the mood at the beginning of *Witch of Blackbird Pond*.
- Adopt a character role to make a presentation about the novel to the class.
- Critique two students' writing for content and style.
- Revise his/her writing as a result of critic input.

Figure 4.16

High School Outcomes
(partial samples at various levels)

I. **Upon graduation the student should be able to:**

- Read literature and news articles accurately and critically.
- Write clearly and effectively for a variety of purposes including communication for business, academic and personal audiences.
- Speak at least two languages well enough to communicate ideas and feelings.
- Use mathematics to solve real-world problems.
- Make decisions based on relevant information and gospel values.

II. **The science department focuses instruction so that students will:**

- Use scientific method and deductive and inductive reasoning to pose questions and generate solutions from collected data.
- Speak accurately about key current concepts of the life and physical sciences.
- Relate scientific knowledge to ecological, environmental, and political issues.

The art department focuses instruction so that students will:

- Exercise creativity in the production of works in the areas of design, graphic/computer design, drawing and painting.
- Evaluate and critique works of art in the light of the basic principles and elements of art.
- Manifest a proficiency in the use of tools and materials related to the particular area of study.
- Relate the characteristics of a work's particular style to a specific period in the history of art.

III. **After completing this course, students will be able to:**

20th Century Authors

- Write effective analyses that are either technical (stylistic), impressionistic (personal responses), or evaluative (critiquing a theme or device).
- Identify various literary techniques used by modern authors including symbol, metaphor, irony, satire, stream of consciousness, and image patterns.
- Argue the validity of certain 20th century themes which include alienation, sexual and racial discrimination, and rebellion against authority, and test those themes against their own experiences.

Honors Algebra I

- Solve equations and inequalities.
- Form general problem solving patterns which he/she can retain and implement with minimum review.
- Solve probability, counting, mixture, age and work problems related to real world situations.
- Graph solutions using number lines, Cartesian coordinates and Venn diagrams.

continued on next page

Figure 4.16 continued

IV. By the end of this unit students will be able to:

20th Century Authors
- Identify sexist beliefs and values, held by the novel's characters, which are reinforced by religious, political and family institutions.
- Explain what is meant by structure and narrative point of view and apply to *The Color Purple*.
- Write an impressionistic analysis of Shug's beliefs about religion and spirituality.

Honors Algebra I
- Graph numbers and set coordinates of points on a number line.
- Use grouping symbols and standard order of operations to simplify and evaluate algebraic expressions.
- Identify and use field properties in simple algebraic proofs.

In a very real way, a teacher's answer to the question, "Why is this part of your instructional design?" should always be, "Because it facilitates the significant learning of our school as articulated in the outcomes."

The bottom of **Figure 4.17** comes at this another way. Instead of using the more specific unit outcome focusing on using supplementary sources, this outcome identifies the performance context in which several student responses demonstrating learning will occur. One of them, "gather information from at least three sources", addresses the graduation, subject area and grade level outcomes above. As reflected on in the first examples, the reason teachers include use of supplementary sources at all is in response to the more broadly stated outcomes.

Figure 4.18 illustrates an example of secondary alignment made apparent through outcomes. Working from the graduation outcome, "Students will make decisions based on relevant information and gospel values," we ask, "How will social studies instruction contribute to achieving this outcome?" The department outcome can be worded as "Students will think critically and make value judgments about the events of social studies." At the course level, we connect this departmental/program level outcome to the specific subject matter of U.S. History and then to the more specific subject matter of a unit within the course.

As in the elementary school example, an important reason why we include *this* outcome in the unit outcomes, rather than a myriad of other possible outcomes, rests on its connection to the course, department and graduation outcomes. If we are serious about graduating students who can make decisions based on relevant information and Gospel values, we must provide teaching/learning situations to coach the learning and we must offer valid opportunities for students to demonstrate progress in and achievement of the stated learning. A useful written curriculum articulates these connections. It provides a bridge for teachers from multidimensional, integrated, highly significant graduation outcomes to unit/weekly teaching decisions.

Summing It Up

Educators face the constant challenge of helping students build effective response patterns to multidimensional situations while interacting with students in relatively small time and space blocks. Often, we succumb to the tendency to focus on the immediate lesson or week of lessons without consciously connecting these to the larger learning we espouse in our philosophy and mission. Articulating clear outcomes at each of the four levels forces us to look for and talk about these connections and then address them deliberately in our decision-making. If a graduation outcome is important, then let's be sure it actually becomes part of the stated learning in our grade level/cluster curriculum, courses and units. Outcomes provide the foundation for doing this.

Figure 4.17

Elementary Alignment

Graduation Outcome:	Students will be able to find the information they need.
Subject Area Outcome:	Science:
	Students will be able to use current and historical scientific materials to research answers to laboratory questions.
Grade Level Outcome:	6th Grade Science:
	Students will use supplementary science books in the school library to interpret and explain their laboratory data.
Unit Outcome:	6th Grade Life Science Unit—Systems:
	Students will use at least 3 supplementary science sources to explain their data and conclusions in addressing the problem: What are the effects of activity on pulse rate?

Unit Outcome: Students will conduct lab experiments on the problem:
What are the effects of activity on pulse rate?
They will:

- state the problem
- gather information from at least 3 sources
- form a hypothesis
- collect data
- organize in charts or graphs
- draw conclusions
- interpret findings in light of research

Figure 4.18

Secondary Alignment

Graduation Outcome:	Students will make decisions based on relevant information and Gospel values.
Subject Area Outcome:	**Social Studies:**
	Students will think critically and make value judgments about the events of social studies.
Course Outcome:	**U.S. History:**
	Students will use skills of social analysis to write reflective/evaluative essays on selected events in the history of the United States.
Unit Outcome:	**U.S. History Unit – Civil Rights 1940–1970:**
	Students will write opinions for an unsettled Supreme Court case involving civil rights, using factual information and Gospel values to support their position.

Chapter Five

 Choosing a Set of Outcomes

Principle 3: Select outcomes that touch both the value-integration plane and the discipline-specific plane.

Clearly, the fulcrum for outcomes-centered curriculum decision-making rests with the outcomes selected. Rich and significant outcomes will more likely lead to rich and significant learning than limited and trivial ones. So, which outcomes? Simple answer: those that promote the most learning, those that provide students with the best opportunity for success in the future. Real answer: those that promote the most learning and provide the most future success *within the context* of which learning we value most.

The definition of learning I find most helpful closely parallels Dewey's approach. Learning means responding effectively to the situation. It implies growth and leads to more learning. **Figure 5.1** presents characteristics of effective adults in four areas of life—citizen, worker, parent, and spouse—as well as a summary of characteristics common to adults who, based on the longitudinal studies of Douglas Heath, have been judged effective in all four areas. If we add one more area, believer/member of a church (**Figure 5.4,** Prism IV), we would have one blueprint upon which to build a set of long term outcomes.

Figure 5.1

Characteristics Successful Adults Have in Common
(descending order of importance)

All roles:

- Caring/compassion
- Honesty/integrity
- Sense of humor
- Openness/self-disclosing
- Tolerance and acceptance

Citizenship:

- Energetic commitment to persevere for a cause
- Caring concern for and tolerance of others
- Problem solving attitudes and skills
- Strong ethical character and ideals

Career/Vocation:

- Adaptive intelligence skills (ability to organize, good judgment, analytic ability)
- Motivational commitment to hard work
- Understanding and managing interpersonal relationships
- Communications skills
- Disciplined knowledge and competence

Parent:

- Personality traits: patience, sense of humor, energy, self-confidence, calmness
- Loving-affectionate attitude
- Ability to create predictable environment
- Emotional communicative skills
- Respect for child's individuality
- Involvement with child
- Teacher with expectations and goals for child
- Problem-solving skills and attitudes

Spouse:

- Loving and trusting relation
- Interpersonal communicative skills
- Shared mutuality of interests
- Motivational commitment to maintaining relationship
- Sense of humor, self-confidence, enthusiasm
- Strong ethical-values commitment

Douglas Heath, Ph.D., *Research on Adult Effectiveness*, 1986.

Figure 5.2

The worker of the future, in addition to having basic skills must also have skills in:

- Organizational effectiveness and leadership
- Creative thinking and problem solving
- Interpersonal relations and teaming
- Listening and speaking well
- Self-esteem and motivation
- Knowing how to learn

Motorola, 1993

Figure 5.3

Five Competencies

Resources: Identifies, organizes, plans, and allocates resources

    A. Time—Selects goal-relevant activities, ranks them, allocates time, and prepares and follows schedules

    B. Money—Uses or prepares budgets, makes forecasts, keeps records, and makes adjustments to meet objectives

    C. Material and Facilities—Acquires, stores, allocates, and uses materials or space efficiently

    D. Human Resources—Assesses skills and distributes work accordingly, evaluates performance and provides feedback

Interpersonal: Works with others

    A. Participates as Member of a Team—contributes to group effort

    B. Teaches Others New Skills

    C. Serves Clients/Customers—works to satisfy customers' expectations

    D. Exercises Leadership—communicates ideas to justify position, persuades, and convinces others, responsibly challenges existing procedures and policies

    E. Negotiates—works toward agreements involving exchange of resources, resolves divergent interests

    F. Works with Diversity—works well with men and women from diverse backgrounds

Information: Acquires and uses information

    A. Acquires and Evaluates Information

    B. Organizes and Maintains Information

    C. Interprets and Communicates Information

    D. Uses Computers to Process Information

Systems: Understands complex inter-relationships

    A. Understands Systems—knows how social, organizational, and technological systems work and operates effectively with them

    B. Monitors and Corrects Performance—distinguishes trends, predicts impacts on system operations, diagnoses deviations in systems' performance and corrects malfunctions

    C. Improves or Designs Systems—suggests modifications to existing systems and develops new or alternative systems to improve performance

Technology: Works with a variety of technologies

    A. Selects Technology—chooses procedures, tools or equipment including computers and related technologies

    B. Applies Technology to Task—Understands overall intent and proper procedures for setup and operation of equipment

    C. Maintains and Troubleshoots Equipment—Prevents, identifies, or solves problems with equipment, including computers and other technologies

"What Work Requires of Schools"
The Secretary's Commission on Achieving Necessary Skills
U.S. Department of Labor, 1991

Figure 5.4

Future Educational Trends/Needs

Prism I: Employment Opportunities

Needed Educational Outcomes:

Students who are able to:

- solve problems
- communicate well
- manage their own learning
- work in groups
- make decisions
- integrate knowledge and skills from different subject areas

Prism II: Adult Effectiveness

Needed Educational Outcomes:

Students who are able to:

- relate well to others
- think flexibly and adaptively
- communicate well
- develop and act on ethical standards
- act with compassion, honesty and tolerance
- exercise disciplined knowledge and skill in a chosen area

Prism III: Whole Earth Health

Needed Educational Outcomes:

Students who are able to:

- integrate knowledge about politics, economics, culture, science, technology, and geography in problem solving and decision making
- speak at least one second language
- see themselves as citizens of the world
- act in ecologically sound ways
- develop and act on personal value systems that include an active sense of the common good, justice, compassion, tolerance, service to others and a commitment to "enough" as opposed to "more"
- eliminate racism and sexism in personal and societal choices

Prism IV: Religious Dimension of Education in a Catholic School

Needed Educational Outcomes:

Students who are able to:

- identify injustice in social institutions and act to change it
- integrate knowledge and faith
- choose a morally sound lifestyle
- use skills of communication and interpersonal relationships to build community
- take responsibility for their own learning
- exercise learning skills and critical judgment in the service of others
- demonstrate growth and maturity in spiritual, liturgical, sacramental, and apostolic life
- use knowledge of scripture, divine revelation and Tradition to discover the person, Jesus Christ
- act to promote justice, peace and good order
- identify and respond with competence and compassion to the needs of others, nationally and internationally
- integrate knowledge from various disciplines in their lives and vocations

Figure 5.2 presents a list of learning skills that Motorola, a corporate leader in employee development, has identified as essential for the worker of the future. Figure 5.3 presents a similar list of learning skills for employees developed by the Department of Labor SCANS group. Figure 5.4 lists learning outcomes suggested by future trends related to employment opportunities, adult effectiveness, membership in a global community, and the religious dimensions of education in a Catholic school. Figure 5.5 lists the National Goals for Education and School and Society Directional Statements from the National Congress on Catholic Schools for the 21st Century. Many of these outcomes overlap. Almost none specify concrete subject matter, much less suggest scope and sequence charts. Certainly, they imply and presuppose discipline-specific learning outcomes, but not in the artificial isolation so often found in schools.

As part of his studies, Heath attempted to correlate school-related factors with effectiveness as an adult. He found that the only school-related factor that correlates positively with adult effectiveness is sustained involvement in extracurricular activities. Extracurricular activities require the integration of knowledge, procedural skills, interpersonal skills, and motivation. They give students the opportunity to act in meaningful ways to effect some product or performance.

Unfortunately, classroom instruction often provides many fewer, if any, such opportunities. In order to fit instruction into neat chunks defined by a set period of time, we have tended to break learning into tiny pieces that become easy to measure and deliver in standard ways to groups of same-age children. This results in school learning that has often become artificial, simplistic, unreal and boring, demanding the lowest level of thinking (recall) and the least natural use of the brain (one-to-one verbal matching).

Many students find such artificial learning no longer motivating, resting as it does on the standard of pleasing the teacher or getting good grades. As Grant Wiggins has commented, "If all our students learn is what's on multiple choice tests, that's not enough." The City of Chicago has a dropout rate of 45%, higher for some populations. Motorola must interview ten people to find one who meets their entry level standards.

Part of the problem lies in the reality that schools still function in an agricultural/ industrial model, rather than an information-age model. Curriculum and school organization tend to focus on development of discrete basic skills and inspection testing "at the end of the line". They ask students to work as individuals on hierarchically sequenced basics that emphasize

Figure 5.5

The National Congress On Catholic Schools
For The Twenty–First Century

School And Society

1. We will educate students to meet the intellectual, social and ethical challenges of living in a technological and global society.
2. We will establish curriculum that acknowledges and incorporates the contributions of men and women of diverse cultures and races.
3. We will educate and challenge our staffs, students, and parents to reject racism, sexism, and discrimination.
4. We will aggressively recruit, retain and develop staff to reflect the needs of an increasingly multi–ethnic, multi–racial and multi–cultural society.
5. We will open new schools and design alternative school models to reflect the changing needs of family, church and society.

The National Education Goals

1. All children will start school ready to learn.
2. The high school graduation rate will increase to at least 90 percent.
3. American students will leave grades 4, 8, and 12 having demonstrated competence in challenging subject matter including English, mathematics, science, history, and geography; and every school in America will ensure that all students learn to use their minds well, so they may be prepared for responsible citizenship, further learning, and productive employment in our modern economy.
4. U.S. students will be first in the world in science and mathematics achievement.
5. Every adult in America will be literate and will possess the knowledge and skills necessary to compete in a global economy and exercise the rights and responsibilities of citizenship.
6. Every school in America will be free of drugs and violence and will offer a disciplined environment conducive to learning.

recitation and recall from short-term memory. They lead to practices by which only some students learn to think. This is not good enough. Educators, parents, legislators are beginning to take seriously the challenge we face: increase the standards for learning in schools *and* commit to providing ALL students with the resources to meet them—knowledge, skills, opportunities for practice and feedback.

Standards have two parts: what and how well. Learning outcomes state the "what" most productively because they focus on student performance. To answer the question of what students should learn, we must begin in the context of learning that is central to the discipline and useful and needed beyond the school walls. In other words, what should students who are able to use the tools of mathematics competently in life and work (as well as school) be able to do? Then we may ask, how will we spiral that learning throughout twelve years of schooling?

The National Council of Teachers of Mathematics (NCTM) is the first professional group to answer these questions about the what of new standards for elementary and secondary school mathematics learning. In their publication, *Curriculum and Evaluation Standards for School Mathematics*, NCTM proposes six broad goals for mathematics education and articulates level outcomes (K-4, 5-8, 9-12) in fourteen categories, including reasoning, problem solving, computation with whole numbers, algebra and statistics. The document says, "Here is what mathematics learning should look like; to do it, we need classrooms where there is less repetition and more invention, less teacher talk and more student talk, less drill and practice on purely routine problems and more opportunity to engage in 'messy' non-routine, real-life problems." It presumes that the mathematics outcomes articulated in the standards are important for all students and that all students can be coached to successful achievement.

The NCTM standards do not constitute a mathematics curriculum for a local school because they do not specify the connections among outcomes, assessments and strategies that should occur at the grade/cluster, course and unit levels. However, they give educators the best place to begin with local curriculum development in mathematics by providing graduation and cluster level program outcomes consistent with the best thinking about learning in mathematics that is both central to the discipline and useful and needed beyond school walls. Working from the broad outcomes, local educators can arrange scope and sequence, articulate more specific enabling outcomes embedded in the broader outcomes, and connect outcomes, assessments and strategies in grades/clusters, courses and units.

Determining what students will learn does not of itself address the issue of how well they must learn it. Outcomes provide a statement of what is to be learned; developing assessment categories, scoring rubrics, and exemplary samples in the context of valid assessment of the outcomes provide the basis for evaluating how well the learning is achieved.

Professional groups in other disciplines have begun working on formulating standards similar to those of the NCTM. **Figure 5.6** lists contact information for standards committees in each discipline and expected completion dates of the projects. **Figure 5.7** lists additional source material being used by the standards committees, and already available for reference. In addition, a set of K-12 learning outcomes for religious education developed by an inter-diocesan task force in the Midwest is included in Chapter Ten, **Figure 10.4**.

The standards developed by these groups promise to be a better source of overall program outcomes than specific textbooks or scope and sequence charts because they seek to formulate learning outcomes that are central to the discipline and useful and needed beyond school. Working from these outcomes and the school's graduation outcomes, teachers can then select textbooks and arrange scope and sequence to facilitate the desired learning, rather than allow a specific textbook to define the learning.

While the outcomes provided by standards committees will provide one good starting point for creating outcomes-centered curriculum, more will be needed to create a curriculum that works for actual students in actual schools. Standards identify the bases to be covered, so to speak. They do not necessarily indicate the relative emphasis, context, or values in which the learning will occur. For dealing with these latter dimensions, the mission and philosophy of the school, future trends, the profile of students, parents and community all play important roles.

Articulating a set of outcomes for a school's curriculum, then, must move forward on two planes. One plane delineates outcomes related to specific disciplines; the other delineates outcomes related to the integration of discipline-specific outcomes within a set of values cherished by the school community. Professional organizations and standards committees (national and diocesan) stand as powerful resources for determining outcomes on the discipline-specific plane. Mission, philosophy, Catholic identity, future trends, parental aspirations, student and community needs all impact the value-integration plane.

In an excellent, high-impact curriculum, the two planes will interact in a dynamic synergy. Graduation outcomes will present a clear vision of how content outcomes should come together in the person of the graduate. Further, these integrating outcomes will give direction to setting priorities and determining emphases in teaching and learning in the specific disciplines. Likewise, the demands of subject area standards will help define the learning community, and thus focus mission and philosophy.

In practice, this means that a local school must develop subject area curriculum in light of professional standards *and* graduation outcomes.

Figure 5.6

Leading Efforts Toward World Class Standards

The Arts

John Mahlmann
Music Educators National Conference*
1902 Association Drive
Reston, Virginia 22091
Projected completion date for World Class
  Standards in the arts: summer 1994.
*(These art standards are being developed in
  coordination with the American Alliance for Theater
  and Education, the National Art Education
  Association, and the National Dance Association.)

Civics

Charles Quigley
Center for Civic Education
5146 Douglas Fir Road
Calabasas, California 91302
Projected completion date for World Class
  Standards in civics: summer 1994.

Geography

Anthony de Souza
Geography Standards Project
National Council of Geographic Education*
1600 M Street, N.W.
Washington, D.C. 20036
Projected completion date for World Class
  Standards in geography: winter 1993.
*(These geography standards are being developed in
  coordination with the Association of American
  Geographers, the National Geographic Society, and the
  American Geographical Society.)

English

Jean Osborn
The Center for the Study of Reading*
174 Children's Research Center
51 Gerty Drive
Champaign, Illinois 61820
Projected completion date for World Class
  Standards in English: fall 1995.
*(These English standards are being developed in
  coordination with the National Council of Teachers of
  English and the International Reading Association.)

Mathematics

The National Council of Teachers of
  Mathematics has already developed World
  Class Standards in mathematics. These
  standards can be used to inform or guide
  the development of local curricula in
  mathematics.

*The National Council of Teachers of
Mathematics Curriculum and Evaluation
Standards*
Order Processing
1906 Association Drive
Reston, Virginia 22091
Item Number: 398E1, ISBN 0–87353–273–2
Cost: $25 each (discounts for bulk orders)

**The following groups are receiving
support from the U.S. Department of
Education to lead the development of
World Class Standards:**

Science

Ken Hoffman
National Academy of Sciences
National Research Council
2101 Constitution Avenue, N.W.
Washington, D.C. 20418
Projected completion date for World Class
  Standards in science: summer 1994.

History

Charlotte Crabtree
**National Center for History in the
  Schools**
University of California at Los Angeles
231 Moore Hall, 405 Hilgard Avenue
Los Angeles, California 90024
Projected completion date for World Class
  Standards in history: spring 1994.

America 2000 Community Notebook
US Government Printing Office: 1992 336–276/70591

Figure 5.7

Documents For Setting Standards Today

National efforts are underway to create World Class Standards in the core subjects. In the meantime, many communities may want to take advantage of standards in some subjects already available.

English

English–Language Arts Framework for California Public Schools, K–12, 1987. Provides teachers, administrators, parents and publishers with an understanding of the State of California's philosophy of English education. It directly relates to English–language arts curriculum standards and guidelines published by the California Department of Education.

California Department of Education
Publicity/Sales Department
P.O. Box 271
Sacramento, California 95812
(916) 445–1260

Supplemental Materials from the California Department of Education

Recommended Readings in Literature, K–8, *Annotated Edition*, 1988.

Recommended Readings in Literature, Grades 9– 12, 1990. Compiled by California teachers, librarians, and administrators to assist local schools in offering diverse, high quality works of literature.

Reading Objectives: 1990 *Assessment*, 1989. *Writing Assessment Framework for the 1994 National Assessment of Educational Progress* (draft), 1992. Objectives being used to develop the National Assessment of Educational Progress in reading. Created by a national consensus process involving reading specialists, curriculum specialists, teachers and school administrators.

Ms. Munira Mwalimu
Aspen Systems, Inc., Suite 701
962 Wayne Avenue
Silver Spring, Maryland 20910
(301) 495–8623

Writing Assessment Framework for the 1994 National Assessment of Educational Progress (draft), 1992. Objectives being used to develop the National Assessment of Educational Progress in writing. Created by a national consensus process involving writing specialists, curriculum specialists, teachers and school administrators.

Ms. Munira Mwalimu
Aspen Systems, Inc., Suite 701
962 Wayne Avenue
Silver Spring, Maryland 20910

Mathematics

Curriculum and Evaluation Standards for School Mathematics, 1989. Created by a national group of experts and teachers of mathematics. Establishes 54 standards for mathematics achievement.

National Council of Teachers of Mathematics
Order Processing
1906 Association Drive
Reston, Virginia 22091
(800) 235–7566, extension 135
Fax: (703) 476–2970

Supplemental Materials from NCTM

Curriculum and Evaluation Standards Addenda Series
Developed to complement the NCTM Standards. Includes 22 volumes, each offering activity suggestions, teacher resources and assessment criteria for specific grade levels and content areas.

Mathematics Framework for California Public Schools, K–12, 1992. Expands upon the 1985 Mathematics Framework. Includes general goals and objectives as well as specific suggestions and alternatives to meet those goals.

California Department of Education
Publicity/Sales Department
P.O. Box 271
Sacramento, California 95812
(916) 445–1260

continued on next page

Figure 5.7 continued

Science

Science for All Americans, 1989.
Published by the American Association for the Advancement of Science. Examines the substance and character of scientific education for all citizens. Defines common knowledge required for scientific literacy.

Oxford University Press
Order Department
2001 Evans Road
Cary, North Carolina 27513
(800) 451–7556

Science Framework for California Public Schools, K–12, 1990.
Provides discussion of pedagogical approaches and processes, such as the scientific method, as well as specific recommendations for systemic reforms in science education, including suggestions for attracting more students to science classes.

California Department of Education
Publicity/Sales Department
P.O. Box 271
Sacramento, California 95812
(916) 445–1260

Science Assessment Framework for the 1994 National Assessment of Educational Progress (draft), 1992.
Objectives being used to develop the National Assessment of Educational Progress in science. Created by a national consensus process involving scientists, curriculum specialists, teachers and school administrators.

Ms. Munira Mwalimu
Aspen Systems, Inc., Suite 701
962 Wayne Avenue
Silver Spring, Maryland 20910
(301) 495–8623

History

History Assessment Framework for the 1994 National Assessment of Educational Progress.
Objectives being used to develop the National Assessment of Educational Progress in history. Created by a national consensus process involving historians, curriculum specialists, teachers and school administrators.

Ms. Munira Mwalimu
Aspen Systems, Inc., Suite 701
962 Wayne Avenue
Silver Spring, Maryland 20910
(301) 495–8623

Building a History Curriculum: Guidelines for Teaching History in Schools, 1988.
Outlines six "Vital Themes" to be considered in the study of history, which can be used in designing and implementing a history curriculum.

National Council for History Education
26915 Westwood Road
Suite B–2
Westlake, Ohio 44145
(216) 835–1776

History–Social Science Framework for California Public Schools, K–12, 1988.
Outlines and organizes historical facts and concepts into a chronological, sequential system. Includes strands on geographic, historical, and civic literacy.

California Department of Education
Publicity/Sales Department
P.O. Box 271
Sacramento, California 95812
(916) 445–1260

Lessons from History: Essential Understandings and Historical Perspectives Students Should Acquire
Written by historians, curriculum leaders and classroom teachers. Identifies historical themes and understandings to be taught in grades K–12. A resource for setting standards and developing assessments, for teachers, curriculum planners, and policy makers.

National Center for History
Attention: Pamela Hamilton
University of California, Los Angeles
Moore Hall 231
405 Hilgard Avenue
Los Angeles, California 90024–1521
(310) 825–4702

Geography

Guidelines for Geography Education: Elementary and Secondary Schools, 1984.
Employs five fundamental themes of

continued on next page

Figure 5.7 continued

geography to serve as guidelines for general geographic concepts, course offerings and student achievement.

National Council for Geography Education
16A Leonard Hall
Indiana University of Pennsylvania
Indiana, Pennsylvania 15705
(412) 357–6290

Supplemental Materials from the NCGE
K–6 *Geography: Themes, Key Ideas and Learning Opportunities*, 1987.
7–12 *Geography: Themes, Key Ideas and Learning Opportunities*, 1989.
Serve as resources for key concepts and actual classroom activities. Expand upon and illustrate examples for implementation of the Guidelines for Geographic Education.

Geography Assessment Framework for the 1994 National Assessment of Educational Progress (draft), 1992.
Objectives being used to develop National Assessment of Educational Progress in geography. Created by a national consensus process involving geographers, curriculum specialists, teachers and school administrators.

Ms. Munira Mwalimu
Aspen Systems, Inc., Suite 701
962 Wayne Avenue
Silver Spring, Maryland 20910
(301) 495–8623

History–Social Science Framework for California Public Schools, K–12, 1988.
Outlines and organizes historical facts and concepts into a chronological, sequential system. Includes strands on historical, geographic, and civic literacy.

California Department of Education
Publicity/Sales Department
P.O. Box 271
Sacramento, California 95812
(916) 445–1260

Civics

CIVITAS: A Framework for Civic Education, 1991.
Developed by the Center for Civic Education and the Council for the Advancement of Citizenship. Designed to guide curriculum designers, teachers, and

administrators as they design a program to enable students to gain an understanding of the fundamental concept of citizenship, and the rights and responsibilities that accompany it.

Maxway Data Corporation
225 W. 34th Street
Suite 1105
New York, New York 10001
(800) 683–0812

History–Social Science Framework for California Public Schools, K–12, 1988.
Outlines and organizes historical facts and concepts into a chronological, sequential system. Includes strands on geographic, historical, and civic literacy.

California Department of Education
Publicity/Sales Department
P.O. Box 271
Sacramento, California 95812
(916) 445–1260

Arts

Visual and Performing Arts Framework for California Public Schools, K–12, 1989.
Provides guidelines for teaching dance, drama/theater, music and the visual arts through instruction in art appreciation and comprehension, as well as student expression.

California Department of Education
Publicity/Sales Department
P.O. Box 271
Sacramento, California 95812
(916) 445–1260

Model Learner Outcomes for Art Education, 1991.
Sets standards for artistic knowledge and abilities for students. Includes evaluation criteria.

Minnesota Curriculum Services Center
70 West County Road B–2
Little Canada, Minnesota 55117
(800) 652–9024
(612) 483–4442

School Music Program: Description and Standards, 1986
Contains philosophy of music education,

continued on next page

Figure 5.7 continued

suggests subject matter mastery levels for students of all ages, and provides administrative and pedagogical standards and methods of implementation.

The Music Educators National Conference
Publicity/Sales Department
1902 Association Drive
Reston, Virginia 22091
(703) 860–4000

Arizona Visual Arts Essential Skills, 1988. Based upon three "quality components" of hands–on "Creative Art Expression," "Aesthetic Assessment" and knowledge of "Art in Cultural Heritage." Suggests ways to integrate art education with other

disciplines.

Arizona Department of Education
Central Distribution Services
1535 West Jefferson
Phoenix, Arizona 85007
(602) 542–4361

Dance Curricula Guidelines for K–12, 1988. Serves as a resource for curriculum design. Includes general foundations for dance education as well as an annotated bibliography of state dance curriculum guidelines.

AAHPERD Publication Sales
1900 Association Drive
Reston, Virginia 22091
(800) 321–0789

AMERICA 2000 Community Notebook

Sometimes, the connection between the two will appear in the statement of the grade/cluster, course or unit outcomes; more often, the connection between subject area standards and graduation outcomes will become fully apparent only in the stated connections among outcomes, assessments, and strategies for a particular piece of the curriculum.

For example, being able to analyze the events of history in terms of their impact on future generations, might constitute a discipline-specific outcome for social studies. The fact that, in one school, students move toward achieving this outcome by working in teams on concrete, multidimensional projects, often focused on social justice issues, might well stem from the mission, philosophy, and charisma of the school community, expressed in graduation outcomes. In another school, with another set of graduation outcomes, the social studies curriculum might specify different kinds of assessments and strategies to teach the same outcome.

Creating an outcomes-centered curriculum that works requires a school to specify the learning on both planes (discipline-specific and values-integrating) as *learning outcomes* rather than *goals*, characteristics of the graduate, or content topics. Further, the Catholic identity of the school and general commitment to academic excellence would seem to require that the full set of outcomes, assessments, and strategies in the curriculum be screened to incorporate the following learning strands: peace and justice, multicultural/gender inclusivity, global awareness, integration of faith and culture, critical and creative thinking, technology, and interpersonal skills.

The High Success Network on Outcomes-Based Restructuring, directed by William Spady, suggests that school districts formulate exit outcomes (values-integrating) in terms of universal dimensions of living: interpersonal relationships, culture and leisure pursuits, environmental reliance, civic and global interdependence, work and resource management, life-long learning, and personal wellness and fulfillment. Underlying these dimensions of living, according to Spady, are fundamental life performance roles that people need to master: users and performers, problem finders and solvers, creators and producers, learners and thinkers, listeners and communicators, teachers and mentors, team members and partners, leaders and organizers. In this framework, the values-integrating exit outcomes (graduation, grade/cluster, perhaps course) would indicate what students should know, do, be like in order to fulfill the life performance roles. Discipline-specific outcomes are selected as enablers for the culminating life performances.

The network of Jesuit high schools has identified five essential characteristics of the graduate: open to growth, intellectually competent, religious, loving, and committed to being just. In Jesuit high schools, these characteristics would form the basis for articulating the graduation outcomes in light of which discipline-centered and other outcomes would be selected.

Summing It Up

In choosing a set of outcomes, a school must: 1) *identify* the important, integrating roles/characteristics/values—the "what is it all for" statements; 2) then *state* these as learning outcomes (how students who know, do, are like that will behave); and 3) then *use* these along with subject area standards to shape the curriculum. For example, if on the value-integration level, a school says it wants students to be committed to transforming the world, a key graduation outcome might be stated this way: Graduates will use knowledge and skills to create responses that make communities more just and peace-filled. The school would then use this outcome to design a culminating assessment that gives students the opportunity to *do this* for some specific community. This outcome and the assessment would then *shape* the rest of the curriculum in clear, challenging, and concrete ways. The shaping will entail articulating "on-the-way-to" outcomes for courses, grade levels, units; designing assessments to demonstrate achievement, both of culminating and enabling outcomes; selecting and using strategies likely to promote the learning stated in the outcomes and demonstrated in the assessments.

References

Curriculum Improvement Process. (1984) Commission on Research and Development, Jesuit Secondary Education Association. 3rd Edition.

Heath, Douglas. (1986) Professor Emeritus, Haverford College. Haverford, PA, Workshop notes.

Motorola University, Motorola, Inc. (1993) 1303 East Algonquin Rd., Schaumburg, IL 60196. Edward W. Bales, Director of Education - External Systems.

Spady, William. The High Success Network on Outcomes-Based Restructuring. (1992) (303) 328-1688.

Wiggins, Grant. (1992) Center on Learning Assessment and School Structuring (CLASS). Genesco, NY

Chapter Six

 ## Designing a More Perfect Match Among Outcomes, Assessments, and Strategies

Principle 4: View the curriculum you will build as a concise statement of the matches you want among outcomes, assessments, and strategies.

Think about something you have learned to do well. How did it happen? Almost certainly, the learning process involved a lot more than reading books about it and listening to presentations by experts. At some point, you became actively engaged in "trying it out" and you received feedback that helped you reinforce and correct your responses. The more closely the feedback connected to what you wanted to learn and to how you were doing at learning it, the more effectively and, probably, more enjoyably, the learning occurred.

I love flowers and flower gardens. For a long time, I wanted to surround my house with flowers, but I had very little knowledge about gardening. Whenever I talked to gardeners and began to read about gardening, I became overwhelmed by the immensity of my lack of knowledge in relation to the seemingly infinite possible gardens I could create. The result: I longed for flowers and did almost nothing.

I had a goal—more flowers—but no outcome. When I finally specified the outcome I wanted (To create a perennial garden in a 50 by 7 foot space in my backyard), I began to make progress in learning how to garden. I read about perennial gardens; I visited perennial gardens; I talked to experienced gardeners about growing perennial flowers; I sought the advice of local nurseries about perennials that flourish in my area. One day, on the train to work, I began sketching possible plant organizations and arrangements. I showed these sketches to others and made changes. Finally, I began to buy plants and put them in the ground. I learned about their care and feeding. I observed their progress and started experimenting with moving plants that weren't flourishing. I am still not an "expert", but I have a beautiful garden and the foundation to continue learning.

Three important things came together for significant learning to occur in my example: a clear sense of the learning I wanted (outcome); the opportunity to try out that learning and assess progress and need for more learning; and appropriate, focused input to build knowledge and skill. **These same three elements form the foundation for a curriculum that works: a clear statement of what is to be learned, opportunity to demonstrate the learning, input and feedback that improve performance.** In more traditional language, a curriculum that works establishes a high degree of congruence among the written curriculum, the tested curriculum, and the taught curriculum. In the language of an output model, a curriculum that works reflects a strong congruence among outcomes, assessments, and teaching/learning strategies arrived at *in that order.* **Figure 6.1** diagrams this congruence.

The **first step** to building congruence consists of formulating learning outcomes. For example, we might formulate this outcome for Spanish I: Students will carry on intelligible conversation in Spanish related to school life, home life and travel. Following the decision-making flow outlined in Chapter Three, **the second step** calls for the design of assessment instruments that give students a valid opportunity to demonstrate the learning. In this case, valid assessments would ask students to converse in Spanish about the topics mentioned in the outcome. Perhaps we would design a series of five and ten minute conversations requiring both predictable and unpredictable responses. In **the third step**, the teacher selects teaching/learning strategies that promote the learning, that coach the students to expected performance in the conversations. These strategies might well include shorter conversations with the teacher and each other, group practice or role play in expected and unexpected situations, as well as structured dialogues and worksheets, all used to give students appropriate feedback to improve performance. The selected assessments and strategies match the outcome and will likely promote high achievement. More powerful learning occurs when such a match exists.

Consider, instead, a teaching/learning situation in which the match does not exist. Suppose a teacher starting from the same outcome used class time for structured oral drills focused on vocabulary and noun/verb agreement, played tapes of formal dialogues presented in the textbook, asked students to memorize and deliver the dialogues, and gave a written test in which students responded to dialogue prompts. The level of learning in this situation would be much more limited than in the first situation. In this scenario, students never practice free-flowing conversation in the same and different situations, so their ability to do so remains problematic at best. At least the test does match the use of class time, even though both the test and the strategies do not match the outcome very well.

A potentially more harmful and unfair situation arises when the assessment does not match the instructional design. What if, in the second scenario above, the teacher used the same strategies in class and then evaluated the students on the basis of free-flowing, ten minute conversations in an unpredicted context? Most likely, students would not do very well; even worse, they would be angry and demoralized.

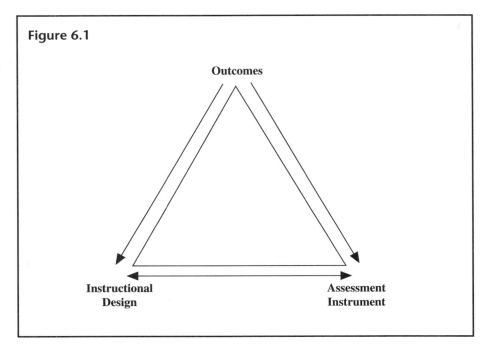

Figure 6.1

Outcomes

Instructional
Design

Assessment
Instrument

Goal statements in curriculum design leave even more room for mismatch. If, instead of the outcome, we began with a goal or topic statement ("foster conversation about school life, home life and travel" or simply "home life, school life, and travel"), the teacher could validly select practically any combination of assessments and strategies that addressed the subject matter in some way. She would have no clear basis for checking the match. Probably, she would teach the materials available (textbook) and test what she taught. The learning might not be significant or well-aligned with the school's stated mission and philosophy. In some instances, the test might not match what was taught because the teacher is too far removed from the learner's level of experience with the subject matter or because the test is designed to find out what the students don't know rather than what they do know.

I recently observed a set of curriculum decisions made by a sixth grade reading teacher relating to vocabulary development. The reading program used literature rather than basal readers; vocabulary to be learned came from the books read by the class. The teacher gave the children a list of vocabulary words for each chapter. They looked up definitions on their own, corrected the definitions together in class, and took a written test matching the word to its meaning after every three chapters. Most children did quite well on the tests. On the test at the end of one of the books, the teacher used some of the vocabulary to ask questions about the book. Many students misunderstood the questions and did not answer them very well, even though they had done quite well on the vocabulary tests.

In this example, two things contributed to a mismatch that resulted in limited, short-term learning. First, the teacher had not articulated a clear outcome. "Vocabulary development" specifies only the subject matter and says nothing about the level of response to the subject matter expected of students. Second, the children practiced and were coached in finding and recognizing the correct definition for each word. When the test matched the teaching, they did well; when the test asked for a different response (use the words correctly in context), the children were unprepared.

Mismatches seriously limit and sometimes undermine learning and perhaps even damage the learner. My daughter had a science teacher whose curriculum decisions generated mismatches regularly. From the students' perspective, the point of the class was to do what the teacher wanted. Usually that meant recalling information on a written test; sometimes the information came from the textbook, sometimes from class notes; sometimes from another book the teacher referred to but never made available to students. Sometimes the terminology on the tests matched the terminology used in class; sometimes it didn't. Sometimes problems followed the patterns of those studied in class and for homework; sometimes the problems reversed procedures as they had been learned and used different terminology and/or units of measure, etc. The teacher never indicated what students should be able to do or why it mattered. She blamed students for not performing consistently but refused to let them use former test corrections to improve learning for the next test. Not surprising, she created a classroom full of cynical students who came to assume they had no control over their learning. The only significant learning in this class had to do with developing coping strategies for dealing with an erratic, authoritarian teacher, not with science.

In many of the workshops I give on outcomes-centered curriculum decision-making, I engage participants in a teaching/learning simulation designed to give them an experience of mismatch among outcomes, assessments, and teaching/learning strategies. Participants read a short article for "homework," and then I teach a short lesson on the topic. We spend "class time" discussing the topic in general and sharing personal experiences, perceptions, and beliefs. We touch on the article only briefly. Finally, the teachers and principals turned "students" take a test requiring very specific, biased recall of information from the article. Only one person out of hundreds has ever received an "A" on the test. No one has received a "B". Many, many fail the test.

We then discuss reactions of these educators to the test. The most common responses include *frustration* over the content of the test and how little it matched their expectations, given what I said about the class and what we actually did; *anger* about trivializing an interesting discussion; a sense of being *cheated or tricked* both because they didn't expect a test and didn't know ahead of time that they should have read the article for tiny details. Some felt they could have done well if they had known what was expected; some felt that the learning represented on the test simply wasn't worth learning.

This simulation makes the point, by way of firsthand experience, that mismatches in curriculum design generate very little significant learning and many negative feelings. Students experience mismatches regularly; yet, teachers often dismiss negative feelings and reactions to what the students consider "unfair" or "dumb" tests. Sometimes the students may be right. Maybe the test truly was unfair because it did not match communicated expectations and/or methods of teaching and learning. Maybe the test was "dumb" in the sense that it did not provide a valid opportunity to demonstrate significant learning (mismatch between outcome and assessment). Maybe the children are genuinely upset because they worked hard and didn't succeed and don't know why.

Teachers who care about learning do not create mismatches deliberately, and yet they occur. Why? I discovered two important things in designing this simulation that suggest an answer to the question.

First, when you begin with clear outcomes, it becomes much more difficult to create a mismatch without knowing it. In designing the simulation, I started with the following outcomes:

Participants will:

1. Experience a mismatch among stated outcomes, assessment and teaching/learning activities.

2. Share feelings and reactions to simulation experience.

3. Redo the lesson to create a match.

To make this happen, I needed to design a "matched" lesson in order to deliberately mismatch it. I discovered how difficult this proved to be. Once I established a reasonable outcome for the simulated lesson, I discovered that possible valid assessments and appropriate instructional strategies to coach performance practically leapt off the page. The teacher in me kept resisting a lesson design that would most likely *not promote* the learning of the lesson. Articulating what I would want students to do to indicate learning made me want to select an assessment that would truly give them an opportunity to do it and strategies that would help them do it well. In other words, once I had followed the curriculum decision-making flow for an output model, it took great concentration to undo it.

The second thing I learned in designing the simulation caught me by surprise. By the time I was ready to use the simulation with a faculty, I *could not tell* whether or not I had created a mismatch. I had set out to create a mismatch and I wasn't sure I had. In fact, I was fairly sure I hadn't; everyone would "ace" the test and the simulation would fail. I had become so familiar with the article and the topic that I could no longer accurately identify what a first-time reader/responder might experience. **My ability to detect a mismatch among outcome, assessment, and strategies (especially between assessment and strategies) decreased as my expertise increased.** The more knowledgeable I became about the subject matter, the less certain I became about likely student response to the test. When I looked over the test prior to the first use of the simulation, I found myself thinking, "Anyone who reads the article will breeze through this test." No one did; the unnerving part was that I thought they would.

A teacher in a later workshop made the point dramatically in response to my insight that expertise can inadvertently contribute to mismatches. She announced that as she was about to teach *Romeo and Juliet*, she realized she had read the play 72 times. How could she possibly recall the likely response of ninth graders reading it for the first time? Without a clear learning outcome as the starting point for her curriculum decisions, she could easily teach the play in ways she had before or ways that seemed to connect with these students or in ways that came out of new insights she had about the play, and then write a test that related more to her knowledge base and experience than to the students' learning based on the coaching she did during this instructional period. And if students did less well on the test than expected, she could attribute it to their lack of effort rather than to a genuine and unhelpful mismatch.

Much of the current focus on school reform comes out of the growing realization that mismatches abound in our schools and seriously limit learning. When we test isolated skills and ask students to recall bits of information, it should not surprise us that students cannot use the information and skills to solve problems or create products, even if we declare these more complex learnings to be the goals of our teaching. When we fill class time with teacher talk, we should not be surprised at limited student communication skills and little evidence of students' thinking for themselves. When we teach subject matter from the textbook, we should not be surprised by lack of application to current experiences and little active connecting to other "subject matter."

The increasing emphasis on performance assessment responds directly to the need for more effective, deliberate matches among the what and the how of learning. If we want students to use math skills and concepts to solve non-routine, real-life problems (outcome), then we must provide legitimate opportunities for them to do exactly that (performance assessments), and we must teach in ways that build acceptable performance (strategies). If we want students to engage in non-violent conflict resolution (outcome), then we must provide opportunities for them to show they can do it (assessments), and select effective ways to coach their performance (strategies).

Summing It Up

Students learn what they need to learn, given enough time and opportunity. They learn at home, on the streets, on the job, from their friends, from TV. What schools ought to have over these other learning situations is speed, focus, and safety. Professional educators in dialogue with the community have the responsibility to provide a clear vision of what the important learnings are and to determine the kinds of experiences students need to develop these learnings. In addition, they must be able to assess when learning has occurred and adapt the learning environment, when needed, to facilitate more learning. The ability to *consciously* bring these three pieces into a positive synergy sets teachers apart from others from whom students learn. Students *should* learn more in schools than they would wandering around the neighborhood. They do so best when teachers build conscious and effective matches among outcomes, assessments, and teaching/learning strategies.

Articulating curriculum from the starting point of learning outcomes is the first step to creating powerful, positive matches that result in greater and more significant learning. The second step is creating assessments that truly match the outcomes and reflect authentic performance. With these two elements in place, teaching/learning strategies selected to promote the learning will fall into place. And since the outcome indicates what *students* will *do* and the assessment gives them the opportunity to do it, effective and useful strategies will necessarily move in the direction of being more student-centered and active.

Chapter Seven:

 ## Developing a Written Curriculum That Supports the Match

Principle 5: In the written curriculum, whatever the format, specify enough and not too much.

Faculty may agree that this way of doing curriculum makes a lot of sense, and still resist writing it down. The presence of a written curriculum, in and of itself, certainly constitutes no proof of excellence. We can all cite classrooms where high levels of learning go on routinely in the absence of a written curriculum. Likewise, we can all point to schools with reams of written curriculum that sit on the shelf in the principal's office and appear only for the benefit of the local accrediting agency. Given a choice, we would certainly prefer the former situation to the latter.

Without a written curriculum, however, the educational program operates on an *ad hoc* basis. Individual teachers may do wonderful things with their students. If they remain at a school for a long time, the program will assume some consistency, particularly if the school is fortunate enough to hold onto a cluster of such teachers and small enough that most students "have" these teachers. What happens when teachers leave? Or when new teachers join the staff? What if things that have worked before begin producing weaker results with new students? What if the state or the diocese insists on incorporating a new strand—critical thinking, parenting, AIDS education, global perspectives, multicultural diversity? What if different teachers who teach the same courses or grade levels/clusters generate very different learning environments and learning experiences so that what students learn in one third grade religion class or eleventh grade ethics course is substantially different from what students in other classes learn? What if a teacher gets sick and requires a long-term substitute? Curriculum that resides almost entirely in the mind of a teacher, offers little help in any of these situations.

Writing down curriculum for the sake of writing it down, also offers little help, because chances are good that such curriculum does not reflect what actually happens in classrooms. **For a local school, creating a curriculum that works means hammering out the important decisions about what students will learn, how they will be assessed on the learning, and what teachers will do to help the learning happen; it means finding a manageable way to communicate these decisions in writing; it means committing to teaching from the written decisions.**

This kind of written curriculum offers a major help to teachers in increasing learning. First of all, it frees the teacher to focus his creative energies and planning time on strategies/materials/activities/resources that will most likely promote greater learning with *these* students. The *what* of learning and much of the *how will I know* clearly appear already in the written document.

Second, this kind of written curriculum provides a solid, long-lasting basis for communication: among professional staff, with parents, with boards, with central offices. Using the written curriculum, educators can periodically review the total learning experiences in any part of the educational program in relation to current thinking and research.

Third, such a written curriculum becomes a highly professional tool for accountability. Educators hold the responsibility for using knowledge and expertise to promote significant and useful learning. It should not remain a mystery to parents and students and other teachers on the staff exactly what that learning will be this year and from year to year. In addition, principals, parents, boards have a right to evidence about whether the intended learning is happening. A written curriculum that connects outcomes, assessments, and strategies allows the discussion of demonstrated achievement of significant learning to occur on more objective ground.

Finally, and perhaps most importantly, a good written curriculum affirms and supports excellent, experienced teachers in what they already do AND provides less experienced, less effective teachers with a scaffold to support growth and improvement, thus insuring more learning for more students.

Selecting the Format

There is no "one right format" or "one right way to it." A written curriculum that supports and communicates a match among outcomes, assessments, and strategies will certainly include at least these three components in some useful arrangement. In addition, schools might find it helpful to also include some specification of subject matter, instructional time frame, and major resources. **Figures** 7.1 and 7.2 suggest elements for inclusion in a written curriculum for secondary and elementary schools. The secondary example assumes an educational program organized into courses (departmental or interdisciplinary) and units within courses; the elementary example assumes that program planning occurs within subject areas on grade or cluster levels or multiple subject areas for interdisciplinary learning and in units or weekly time frames.

Figure 7.1

Secondary Curriculum

1. Mission/Philosophy
2. Graduation Outcomes
   Culminating Performances
3. Departmental/Subject Area Outcomes
4. Course Syllabi:
   Course Title
   Course Description/Goals (Optional)
   Course Outcomes
   Course Assessments/Culminating Performances
   Units:
      Content/Subject Matter
      Unit Outcomes
      Sample Assessments
      Suggested Strategies
      Approximate Time
      Major Resources

Figure 7.2

Elementary Curriculum

1. Mission/Philosophy

2. Graduation Outcomes
   Culminating Performances

3. Subject Area Outcomes
   (K–8 or K–2, 3–5, 6–8 or K–4, 5–8)

4. Grade Level/Cluster Subject Area Outcomes
   (Depending on organization of school and #3 above)

   Grade Level/Cluster Assessments
   (Culminating Performances)

5. Units:

         Content/Subject Matter
         Unit Outcomes
         Sample Assessments
         Suggested Strategies
         Approximate Time
         Major Resources

   Or   Weekly Subject Area Plans:
         Content/Subject Matter
         Grade Level Outcomes to be worked on
         Assessment Task(s)
         (Suggested Strategies)→→→ In Teacher's
         (Major Resources)   Daily Plan Book

Whatever the arrangement of the written curriculum, the primary operating principle must be to **provide enough detail in easily usable form for teachers to use the curriculum and make connections among outcomes, assessments, and strategies/materials in their teaching**. A useful written curriculum makes it unnecessary for teachers to flip back and forth between sections and/or documents in order to determine outcomes, assessments, and/or likely materials/activities/resources for *this unit*. A useful written curriculum also makes it unnecessary for each teacher to create outcomes, assessments and strategies/resources *for a unit* each time the unit begins.

For a curriculum to work and increase learning for more students, it must map the essential curriculum decisions teachers will use, and the *teachers must use it*. If we are convinced that connecting outcomes, assessments, and strategies will increase learning, then a useful written curriculum will spell

---

Figure 7.3

7th Grade Language Arts

Unit: Writing

1. Sentences
   - Types
   - Kinds
   - Parts
2. Punctuation and Spelling
3. Paragraphs
   - Topic Sentence
   - Main Idea
4. Writing Process
5. Kinds of Writing

Text:

Time: 2–3 periods per week.

---

out these intended connections in a way that enables teachers to use it to plan every instructional period. A school's written curriculum *will not include individual lessons.* A school's written curriculum *should be the immediate source* for all planning, including individual lessons.

The main problem with most written curriculum is that it focuses on content rather than learning. The statement of curriculum in **Figure 7.3** illustrates this emphasis for a section of 7th grade language arts. This document gives the teacher virtually no help in selecting significant learning outcomes, appropriate assessment tools, and effective teaching/learning activities. One teacher could use grammar exercises, punctuation exercises and weekly structured writing assignments to develop and test specific knowledge and skills listed in the curriculum outline. Another teacher could embed the same knowledge and skills in a learning environment much more akin to a whole language approach. If there is any reason to prefer one teaching/learning situation to the other, this statement of curriculum is useless. In addition, this curriculum gives no indication about any *learning* for which the teacher is accountable. (Graduation outcomes ought to provide the most compelling reason to prefer one teaching/learning situation to another.)

Figure 7.4 presents the same subject matter in a curriculum statement that specifies some clear connections among learning outcomes, assessments,

Figure 7.4

7th Grade Language Arts

Unit:	**Writing**
Subject Matter:	1. Sentence Types
	2. Punctuation, Grammar and Spelling
	3. Paragraph Construction
	4. Writing Process
	5. Kinds of Writing
Outcomes:	1. Students will use correct spelling, punctuation, and grammar in written work
	2. Students will identify types and kinds of sentences and use them in their writing.
	3. Students will write effective narrative, descriptive, expository and persuasive paragraphs following the write, evaluate, edit and rewrite process.
Sample Assessments:	1. As a member of a writing development and critique group, student will generate ideas, write paragraphs, evaluate for content, expression and form; evaluate, edit, and rewrite.
	2. Student will assemble a portfolio of best work in narrative, expository, descriptive and persuasive writing.
	3. Student writing groups will select one grammar/ mechanics point to teach to the class each week.

and strategies. Using this document, the teacher has some clear ideas about what learning to facilitate and the overall context in which to assess and teach it. Daily lessons are not spelled out; nor is the specific order of presentation; nor are the specific prompts for the writing assignments. In a school with this stated curriculum, individual teachers could still create unique classrooms. What would remain constant is the expected and assessed learning (outcomes and assessment types) and, to some extent, the teaching/ learning activities needed to promote achievement of the outcomes.

A word about teaching/learning strategies. Effective teachers use a variety of teaching strategies and learning activities. The very fact that a variety of strategies appear in effective classrooms reflects what we know about how learning occurs. These teachers harness the *full power* of using a variety of strategies, however, when they select the strategies in relation to the intended learning as well as in relation to different learning styles and preferences. Without question, many different strategies will suit a given out-come. Thus, in addition to fitting the outcome, the strategies and activities for a specific instructional situation will also reflect teacher preference, edu-cational philosophy, available materials and resources, student interest and learning styles.

Clearly, if learning outcomes are the driving force for curriculum deci-sion-making, some strategies will be inappropriate and/or inadequate to promote the learning. A number of strategies will be appropriate and effec-tive. The extent to which a school specifies strategies in the written curricu-lum will depend on the importance of the particular strategy to the total learning of the particular outcome and the importance of the learning pro-cess reflected in the particular strategy. Weighing importance here relates directly to the values and priorities established for the school in its mission and philosophy, and graduation outcomes.

One of the biggest decisions local educators face in creating a curricu-lum that works comes down to this: How much do you specify and where do you specify it? The answer: enough and not too much. Enough so that teachers know what students will learn, how they will demonstrate the learn-ing, and what kinds of things teachers must do to help it happen. And enough so that teachers will know these things close to their actual teach-ing. Not too much so that creativity, flexibility and style are stifled.

On the way to a written curriculum that specifies enough and not too much, local educators will need to do research, articulate beliefs about teach-ing and learning, assess needs and observe successful programs. These addi-tional pieces serve as a useful backdrop or context within which the school makes decisions about outcomes, assessments, and strategies. Research find-ings, beliefs about learning and teaching, etc. may be written down as a resource to new faculty, board members or parents in order to help them understand the rationale for what the curriculum itself includes. However, the *working* part of the written curriculum, if it is to be a curriculum that works, must be concise enough for teachers to use every day; concise enough to articulate the non-negotiable connections among learning outcomes, as-sessments, and strategies so that these will in fact shape instruction. In over-simplified terms, the key to a curriculum that works rests with including the right categories of information in a form that matches the way teachers plan and teach in the school.

Figures 7.5 and 7.6 illustrate the "enough and not too much" principle for a unit in high school biology. The statement of curriculum in **Figure** 7.5

gives the teacher not enough information. It represents a generalized statement of content; no indication of expected learning or assessment, and thus no learning-based context for selecting appropriate teaching strategies and learning activities. The statement of curriculum in **Figure** 7.6 connects learning outcomes, assessments and strategies/resources for the same subject matter.

Working from this latter document, the teacher knows what students who have achieved the significant learning of the unit should be able to do; she knows the kinds of opportunities she will use to assess the achievement; and she has some ideas about likely strategies to promote the learning and possible resources. She must still decide which resources to use with each group of students, in what order to present information and practice skills, what kinds of formative processes and assignments she will use to coach students in preparation for the larger assessment tasks.

Even though this statement of curriculum adheres fairly well to the "enough and not too much" principle, we can use it to raise some important issues regarding the central concern identified earlier—how much do you specify and where? Consider the first outcome in **Figure** 7.6. Students could certainly "demonstrate understanding of the parts of the respiratory system and of its functioning and disfunctioning" without constructing a model (assessment #2). Many things are gained by specifying model construction as one of the expected assessments. Constructing a model and using it to demonstrate function and disfunction engages students in multidimensional, hands-on, active learning—hallmarks of learning that lasts and transfers. Model construction makes use of kinesthetic and spatial intelligence as well as logico-mathematical intelligence. It calls for creative thinking and problem-solving, important skills to teach early and often.

Other valid assessments of this outcome (for example, a paper or an oral presentation or a museum exhibit) would teach and test different learning skills and processes, working with the same knowledge and information about the respiratory system. When should the local curriculum specify "construct a model" and when not? There is no easy formula for answering the question beforehand. Writing a curriculum that works will remain a professional and highly creative endeavor precisely because articulating important connections among outcomes, assessments and strategies requires setting priorities which are always rooted in values as well as in knowledge and expertise.

If we specify nothing about manner of assessment (list outcome #1 without indicating any assessments), we take a giant step back from creating a

---

Figure 7.5

High School Biology

Unit: Respiratory System

1. Respiratory System
   - Parts
   - Functioning
2. Respiratory Disorders
3. Environmental Factors Affecting Respiration

Text:

Approximate Time: 8 – 10 days

---

curriculum that works because we have lost an articulated connection between the content of the learning and the expression of that learning. We see the full import of the content of learning only in the expressions of the learning. It *does* make a difference if we use an expository paper to gauge understanding rather than if we use a constructed model. Sometimes the difference will be small and/or not critical to the essential learning; if so, less specification will suffice. Sometimes the difference is great in terms of depth, breadth, and character of desired learning; if so, greater specification is required.

Some educators prefer to regard an outcome as a general behavior or ability that can be developed over time, not a specific task (e.g. ability to speak precisely and accurately about scientific concepts and principles). This approach to outcomes is helpful in keeping curriculum focused on significant learning rather than on a string of discrete behaviors. This approach also makes it possible to develop one set of outcomes that apply at every level, K-8 or K-12. We must keep in mind, however, that outcomes are *observed* and *assessed* in specific tasks and situations. Outcomes and appropriate assessments must appear together in a curriculum that works.

Extended Examples

Consider the partial Algebra I syllabus in **Figure** 7.7. The general course outcomes relate to the subject matter of Algebra I and are consistent with the school's departmental outcomes (**Figure** 7.8) and the NCTM standards. The sample unit specifies learning outcomes for lines and distance, consistent with and working toward the general course outcomes, but more specific in relation to the specific subject matter of the unit. Sample assess-

Figure 7.6

High School Biology

Unit: **Respiratory System**

Subject Matter: 1. Parts of the Respiratory System
                 2. Functioning of Respiratory System
                 3. Respiratory Disorders
                 4. Environmental Factors Affecting Respiration

Outcomes: 1. Students will demonstrate understanding of the parts of the respiratory system and of its functioning and disfunctioning.
                 2. Students will relate environmental and other factors to the proper functioning of the respiratory system.

Sample Assessments: 1. Student will pass an objective test on important terminology and concepts.
                 2. The student will construct a model of the respiratory system and demonstrate how various respiratory disorders interfere with its functioning.
                 3. The student will predict the effects of various factors on the respiratory system, including air quality, exercise, diet and emotions and will evaluate how his current lifestyle will impact long–term respiratory health.
                 4. Working in a lab team, the student will design and conduct an experiment demonstrating the effects on respiratory health of one environmental factor present in his community.

Suggested Teaching Strategies: 1. Cooperative groups to explore effects of factors on respiratory system.
                 2. Mini–lectures on concepts
                 3. Partners for learning terms
                 4. Lab teams
                 5. Role–play of system functioning

Approximate Time: 10 days

Possible Resources: 1. Text:
                 2. CD ROM: simulations
                 3. 3–dimensional model
                 4. Reference shelf materials on respiratory and circulatory systems

ments follow the unit outcomes. These assessments represent specific tasks that students who have achieved the learning stated in the outcomes should be able to do. Suggested strategies identify some teaching/learning activities which are likely to promote the learning of the unit and which are compatible with the department's overall commitment to the teaching principles outlined in the NCTM standards and those suggested by the textbook being used.

Working from this written curriculum, the teacher has a pretty clear idea of what learning he is after regarding lines and distance, and he has a clear idea of the kinds of problems/tasks he will use to determine whether the learning has occurred. In order to prepare his students for these problems/ tasks, he must create a fairly active classroom in which students work together to solve problems connected to real life applications, along with building facility in the use of appropriate technology, mathematical symbols and graphs. His daily planning will involve selecting and arranging presentations, examples, sample problems and experiences that build students' understanding and skills in preparation for the unit assessments, and give him feedback on students' progress. Different teachers using this written curriculum will still create different classrooms. However, the character and quality of the learning in relation to the subject matter will more likely remain constant from classroom to classroom and year to year with such a written curriculum in place.

Written curriculum does not aim to create a "teacher-proof" formula for instruction. Rather, a good written curriculum posits the school's most deeply held convictions about significant learning in an area in such a way that teachers can use it to make instructional decisions that will positively impact learning.

Figure 7.9 presents a partial sample of written curriculum for Grade 5 Mathematics set in the context of K-8 Mathematics goals and outcomes. The goals come straight from the NCTM standards; the K-8 outcomes relate to the mathematics outcomes for the State of Kentucky as adapted by the Archdiocese of Louisville. Grade level outcomes are identified for each of the fifteen K-8 outcomes. (Two sets of grade level outcomes appear in this sample.) The grade level outcomes connect the K-8 outcomes to the specific subject matter designated for Grade 5.

Figure 7.7

Algebra I

Course Outcomes:

By the end of this course, students will be able to:

1. Represent situations using variable expressions, equations, and inequalities.
2. Use problem solving strategies both intuitively and through guided practice.
3. Read mathematics related to Algebra I.
4. Relate real world problems to mathematical strategies.
5. Recognize equivalent representations of the same concept.
6. Make and test conjectures.
7. Translate among symbolic and graphical representations of functions.
8. Formulate math definitions and express generalizations discussed through investigation.
9. Express mathematical ideas orally and in writing.
10. Select and use appropriate technology to solve problems using the mathematics of Algebra I.

Major Resources:

1. Usiskin, McConnell, Brown, Eddings. UCSMP Algebra. Scott Foresmann, 1990.
2. Pollack, Usiskin, Bell, et al. A Sourcebook of Applications of School Mathematics. National Council of Teachers of Mathematics, 1980.
3. Dalton, Leroy. Algebra in the Real World - 38 Enrichment Lessons for Algebra 2. Dale Seymour Publications, 1983.
4. Applications in School Mathematics, NCTM yearbook, 1979.
5. The Ideas of Algebra, K-12, NCTM yearbook, 1988.

Unit Five: Lines and Distance

A. Subject Matter

1. Graphing Lines
2. Horizontal and Vertical Lines
3. Distance and Absolute Value
4. Square Roots
5. Pythagorean Theorem
6. Square Root of Products
7. Distances in the Planes
8. Chunking

B. Outcomes

Students will be able to:

1. Graph straight lines by plotting points.
2. Graph horizontal and vertical lines by ordered pairs (x, k) and (k, y).
3. Find absolute values.
4. Find distance on a number line.
5. Solve absolute value equations and inequalities.
6. Evaluate and simplify expressions involving square roots.
7. Solve equations involving squares and square roots.
8. Use squares and square roots in measurement problems.
9. Use Pythagorean Theorem in finding lengths of the sides of a right triangle.

continued on next page

Figure 7.7 continued

10. Evaluate and simplify expressions involving square roots.
11. Find distance between 2 points in a plane.
12. Evaluate expressions and solve equations by using chunking.
13. Apply Pythagorean Theorem in real life situations.
14. Write their own problems using Pythagorean Theorem.

C. Sample Assessments

1. Meagan's family saved $2000 for a vacation. They spent $250 per day while on vacation.

    a) Write an equation showing how many dollars d the family had left after n days.

    b) Graph all reasonable solutions to your equation in part a. Be sure to label and number the axes.

2. True or false. In the coordinate plane, points on the line y = 100 can have any real number for their coordinate. Explain your answer and graph y = 100.

3. Solve and graph on a number line.

    a) 1 - 10 + x1 = 75

    b) Find the distance between the two points you found in (a).

4. Graph the solutions:

    a) x - 8<4

    b) s - 8>4

5. A ladder 10 m. long rests against the sill of a 2nd story window. The base of the ladder is on the ground 500 cm. from the base of the wall.

    a) Draw a diagram for the above information.

    b) Estimate the height of the 2nd story window.

    c) Find height by the Pythagorean Theorem and express in simplest radical form.

    d) Use calculator to find height.

6. Draw a right triangle on a coordinate plane and use it to find CD if C = (-2, 5) and D = (4, -8).

7. Find (by chunking) 8x - 3 if 4x = 5.5.

8. The neighborhood children always take the shortcut pictured below. Their parents stay on the sidewalk. About how much farther do the parents walk? (Round your answer to the nearest foot.)

9. Have students in groups of two or three develop problems of their own that require the use of the Pythagorean Theorem, similar to the problems in (5) and (8).

D. Strategies

Students:

1. Work in groups.
2. Use technologies.
3. Explain their thinking and problem solving processes to each other.
4. If possible, do an outdoor application involving the computation of distance.

E. Approximate Time

11-13 days

Academy of Our Lady Team, Richard Stalmack-consultant

Figure 7.8

Department: Mathematics

The Department of Mathematics focuses instruction so that students will:

1. Apply mathematical techniques in the solution of real life problems.

2. Demonstrate familiarity with the language and notation of mathematics and express quantitative ideas with precision.

3. Qualify for admission into entry level college math courses.

4. Apply analytical reasoning to problem solving situations.

5. Demonstrate knowledge of algebra and geometry.

In this school, teachers do weekly planning by subject areas, rather than planning in topical or thematic units. The written curriculum reflects this by indicating outcomes and assessment tasks for one week of mathematics instruction. The instructional strategies appear in the teacher's daily lesson plans, along with daily objectives, assessments, and assignments. The daily lesson plans belong to the teacher or group of teachers who choose to use them; they do *not* belong in the school's written curriculum. The written curriculum for Grade 5 would include only the grade level outcomes and the weekly indication of outcomes and assessment.

Different teachers could develop different lesson plans to teach the stated outcomes for the week and prepare students for the assessment event. However, working from this written curriculum, a teacher would have a clear idea of the math learning she is after this week and the task she will use to let children demonstrate the learning. Her creative energy and planning time can go into the how rather than the what of learning. In addition, using this kind of written curriculum brings a high level of consistency about the character and quality of math learning in the school, from teacher to teacher within grade level/clusters and from grade level to grade level.

Figure 7.10 suggests a different format for developing an elementary school curriculum, where instructional planning occurs in topical or thematic units, rather than in weekly chunks. The first page identifies the broad content of the units to be taught. For each unit, teachers specify outcomes, assessments, and suggested strategies (page two). These unit sheets, along with grade level/cluster outcomes for the subject areas, constitute the written curriculum. Teachers will develop daily lesson plans to help children achieve the unit outcomes as demonstrated in the assessments.

Figure 7.9

K–8 Mathematics

Goals

The mathematics curriculum has, as a central aim, developing in students the mathematical "power" needed for today's society. Toward this end, the K–8 curriculum articulates five goals essential to all students, that they:

- Become mathematical problem solvers,
- Learn to communicate about mathematical ideas,
- Learn to reason logically,
- Connect mathematical processes both in and out of the study of mathematics, and
- Readily use estimation and mental computation in a variety of situations.

Outcomes

These essential goals are explicitly stated in the following Archdiocesan Valued Outcomes for Mathematics:

Students will be able to:

Process Strands:

I.   Use problem solving strategies successfully
II.   Communicate mathematical ideas orally and in writing
III.   Display sound mathematical reasoning
IV.   Connect mathematics to real life situations
V.   Use mental math skills and estimate accurately
VI.   Make appropriate and ongoing use of calculators and computers
VII.   Use manipulatives for understanding

Content Strands:

VIII. Use number sense, numeration, and number theory correctly
IX.   Demonstrate an understanding of whole number operations and computation
X.   Display understanding of geometry and spacial concepts
XI.   Use measurement, time, money concepts properly
XII.   Demonstrate an understanding of probability and statistics
XIII. Demonstrate an understanding of patterns, relations and functions
XIV.   Demonstrate an understanding of rational number concepts (fractions/decimals)
XV.   Demonstrate an understanding of algebraic concepts

Mathematics Outcomes: Grade 5
(Partial Sample)

K–8 Outcome V: Use mental math skills and estimate accurately

Students should be able to:

1.   Use a variety of estimation strategies;
2.   Determine when an estimate is appropriate;
3.   Use estimation to determine the reasonableness of results and as an aid in selecting a method for exact calculation;
4.   Apply estimating in working with quantities, measurement, computation, and problem solving; and

continued on next page

Figure 7.9 continued

5.   Use mental arithmetic for all simple operations and for manipulations.

K–8 Outcome IX: Demonstrate an understanding of whole number operations and computation.

Students should be able to:

1.   Demonstrate understanding of how the basic arithmetic operations are related to one another.
2.   Multiply using basic facts through 12's (use mental arithmetic mnemonics, such as the sum of the digits of multiples of 9 is divisible by 9).
3.   Divide using basic facts through 12's.
4.   Multiply a 2–digit number by a 2–digit number without a calculator.
5.   Divide a 2– or 3– digit number by a 1– or 2– digit number with and without a calculator.
6.   Solve one–step story problems using addition, subtraction, multiplication, or division of whole numbers.
7.   Identify the correct operation needed to solve a story problem.
8.   Identify and apply the following properties of addition and multiplication: commutive, associative, property of 0, property of 1, distributive.
9.   Maintain immediate recall of addition and subtraction facts (speed and accuracy).
10.   Demonstrate immediate recall of multiplication and division facts (speed and accuracy) to 12's.
11.   Maintain competence in addition and subtraction of whole numbers with and without regrouping.

Weekly (Unit) Planning: Grade 5 Mathematics

A.   Outcomes: 1. Problem solving (I – 2, 3)
                       2. Estimation (V – 3, 4)
                       3. Number operations and computations (IX – 2, 4, 6, 7,10)

B.   Performance Event/Assessment:

Task:

Part (1)   There are 14 classrooms in St. Peter's School. The maximum number of desks in each classroom is 29. How many students attend the school if it is filled to capacity? a.   What number operation is most effective in solving this problem?

            b. Solve the problem using paper and pencil.

Part (2)   Fold an 8 1/2 by 11 sheet of paper to illustrate the classroom layout. Use numbers to indicate the maximum number of desks in each room. Using only the folded paper estimate the following:

If 3 classrooms are closed, what is the school's greatest possible attendance? Record your estimation.

Use paper and pencil to write the process mathematically.

Compare your estimation with this answer.

Compare your answer with the answer you found in Part (1). Are both answers reasonable? Why?

continued on next page

Figure 7.9 continued

Performance Criteria   Rubric

Ability to determine reasonableness of answer	1 pt.
Correct mathematical computation	2 pt.
Ability to illustrate the word problem using folded paper	1 pt.
Correct mathematical operation utilized	1 pt.
Total	5 pt.

Weekly (Unit) Planning

III.   Instructional Strategies (Sample Teacher's Lesson Plans)

Outcomes-based lesson planning utilizes the adopted textbook as a resource rather than a total instructional program. The week's lesson planning illustrates this blend. Daily objectives which rely on the use of textbook are indicated with an *.

Day (1)

Objective:	To practice multiplying basic facts through 12's
Procedure:	Small group Multiplication BINGO
Materials:	BINGO cards, counters
Assessment:	Teacher observation
Homework:	Home drill on multiplication facts

Day (2)

Objective:	To multiply two 2–digit numbers
*Procedure:	As outlined in text pp. 148 and 149
Materials:	Manipulatives and texts
Assessment:	"Try out" p. 148
Homework:	Extra practice p.171

Day (3)

Objective:	To multiply a 2–digit number (real life application)
Procedure:	Cooperative task with activity card (one per group) found in teacher's resource guide.
Materials:	Construction paper and markers
Assessment:	Cross group critique of finished products
Homework:	Design a problem requiring the multiplication of two 2–digit numbers. Solve your problem.

Day (4)

Objective:	Finding needed information in order to solve problems
*Procedure:	Whole class sharing of homework problems p. 150 of text.
Materials:	Chalk board, individual slates, and calculator
Assessment:	Teacher observation
Homework:	Problems 8, 11, 12 and 16

Day (5)

Objective:	To conduct performance event assessments
Procedure:	Review week's work
	Explanation of task and rubric
	Independent completion of the task
	Materials: Task sheets, scrap paper, (1) 8 1/2 x 11 sheet of paper

Adapted from Archdiocese of Louisville, *Curriculum Framework of Indicators*, Jane Leitner, Archdiocese of Louisville, 1992

Figure 7.10

Topic/Theme/Concept	Topic/Theme/Concept	Topic/Theme/Concept	Topic/Theme/Concept

Topic/Theme/Concept	Subject Area(s)	Topic/Theme/Concept

Topic/Theme/Concept		Topic/Theme/Concept

Topic/Theme/Concept	Topic/Theme/Concept	Topic/Theme/Concept	Topic/Theme/Concept

Lead Teacher _____ Grade _____ Dates to Teach _____

Subject(s) _____ Theme/Unit/Concept _____

Outcomes _____
_____
_____
_____

Assessment _____
_____
_____
_____

Suggested Teacher Activities	Suggested Student Activities	Materials

Adapted from Archdiocese of Dubuque

Lesson plans may well vary from teacher to teacher; unit outcomes and assessments will remain constant for all children.

Figure 7.11 provides a sample syllabus for an independent study secondary English course. The essential connections for a curriculum that works are present: learning outcomes and assessment tasks. Working from this document, both teacher and student have a clear idea of what the student will do to demonstrate significant learning in the course. Since the course calls for independent study, units and teaching strategies are not specified. If this independent study became a regular semester course, the syllabus as presented would be a much weaker example of a written curriculum that supports a match among outcomes, assessments, and strategies precisely because it does not specify units and teaching strategies and thus provides considerably less support for teachers in decision-making.

Figure 7.12 presents a sample written curriculum connecting outcomes, assessments and strategies for an interdisciplinary unit within a high school American Studies course. **Figure 7.13** presents a partial sample of a high school Ethics course. Included are course outcomes, culminating assessments and unit content blocks which the Religious Studies Department will gradually articulate in terms of unit outcomes, key unit assessments and major strategies and materials. This sample is especially helpful in illustrating the way schools can begin serious outcomes-centered curriculum development that can immediately affect teaching and learning and, at the same time, can allow for faculty collaboration over a realistic time span. It is important to note that not all assessments for the course are specified, only those that the school determines must be part of every student's learning experience in Ethics. Finally, **Figure 7.14** presents a sample written curriculum connecting outcomes, assessments and strategies for an interdisciplinary unit on the primary level.

While none of the formats in these extended examples perfectly fit every school or instructional situation, they each respect the core principle for creating a curriculum that works: enough information for teachers to make decisions that lead to the desired learning and not too much information that encourages disregarding the curriculum and/or stifles creativity.

Designing the Curriculum Writing Process

Once the school has embraced an outcomes-centered mindset and a format has been selected, action planning can take place to decide on the order of events and a reasonable time frame for completion.

Figure 7.11

English Independent Study
One Semester Syllabus
Course Title: A Study Of The Black Humanities

Course Description: This independent study course emphasizes the role of Blacks in the areas of American literature, music, and art. Research, oral discussion, written assignments, and periodic attendance at concerts and art museums are requisites for successful completion of this course.

Student Outcomes: After successful completion of this course, the student will be able to:

1. Identify prominent Black authors and poets and their work.
2. Analyze the literature studied in terms of five–part structure: plot, theme, character, setting, conflict.
3. Demonstrate competence in reading comprehension and analysis of selected works, and be able to relate the literature studied in terms of one's own experience and knowledge.
4. Complete a research paper that supports a particular thesis or point of view. Assigned literary works, art exhibits, and musical events will be used to support the thesis. The student will show competence in the use of supporting data, quotations, footnotes, and bibliography.
5. Identify prominent Black artists and their works.
6. Complete a contrast/comparison paper of Black artists.
7. Identify and discuss ways in which the Black humanities have influenced American art, music, and literature.

Course Assessments: The following will be required for successful completion of this course:

1. Research paper consisting of 4–6 typewritten pages
2. Read 3–5 literary works that emphasize Black experiences, including such topics as slavery, civil rights, racism, and Black leadership
3. Completion of a 3–5 page comparison–contrast paper
4. 20–25 hours of oral discussion and presentation of material covered with the instructor
5. Attendance at 2–3 musical concerts that feature Black artists. Either an oral or written report on concerts attended is required
6. Visit to the DuSable Museum of African–American History, accompanied by oral–written report
7. Study of 3–5 prominent Black poets, including discussion and interpretation of their works

Suggested Course Materials: Materials needed to complete the course assignment may be selected from the following:

Literature

Alex Haley – *Roots*
Alice Walker—*The Color Purple*
Gwendolyn Brooks—poetry
Lorraine Hansberry – poetry, novels
James Baldwin
Countee Cullen—poetry, novel (*Color, Copper Sun*)
Gordon Parks—*The Learning Tree*
John Griffin—*Black Like Me*
Martin Luther King—"I Have a Dream"
Richard Wright – *Black Boy, Native Son*
Maya Angelou – *I Know Why the Caged Bird Sings*
Harriett Beacher Stowe – *Uncle Tom's Cabin*

Music	Clubs
Aretha Franklin	Blue Chicago
Miles Davis	Kingston Mines
Quincy Jones	New Checkerboard
Gladys Knight	Lounge
Ray Charles	Jazz Clubs
Andre Crouch	DuSable Museum of
Stevie Wonder	African-American
Michael Jackson	History

Don Madsen

Figure 7.12

American Studies
Interdisciplinary Unit: Individual and Society

Outcomes:

Students will:

1. Analyze acts of civil disobedience in order to articulate the tension that exists between individuals and the demands placed upon them by society.

2. Justify acts of civil disobedience in a variety of situations, based on democratic principles and Gospel values.

3. Construct an informed opinion about the significance of the individual and his/her rights within the context of the U.S. political system.

Assessments:

1. Make a visual presentation that describes the role of conscience in political behavior.

2. Formulate a working definition of civil disobedience.

3. In cooperative groups, develop criteria for justified law–breaking. Defend your criteria in light of appropriate resources such as civil disobedience scenarios studied in class, Church's social teaching, Gospel values, U.S. Constitution, and the Declaration of Independence.

4. Read accounts of the My Lai Massacre in Vietnam and excerpts from Lt. Calley's testimony. Write an essay arguing what Lt. Calley or the men in his command should have done in the situation, and justifying the action under the law.

Suggested Strategies:

1. Discuss civil disobedience scenarios in small groups.

2. Discuss the concept of the individual presented by Emerson, Thoreau, Martin Luther King, and Jesus.

3. Watch the film, *Obedience,* and discuss when an individual is justified in disobeying authority, if ever.

4. Locate possible examples of civil disobedience in current news.

Materials:

1. Ralph Waldo Emerson, "Self–Reliance"

2. Film, *Obedience*, 1969

3. Martin Luther King, "Letter from Birmingham City Jail"

4. Henry David Thoreau, "Civil Disobedience"

5. Civil disobedience scenarios

6. Reference packet on My Lai

Figure 7.13

Course Title: Ethics

Course Description: This course introduces students to the Catholic ethical tradition. Through the study of various ethical philosophies and methodologies, students develop the critical skills necessary to make an informed ethical decision. In this way, students are challenged to examine their own decision–making process. As a result, students come to a deeper appreciation of the various factors involved in the formation of conscience. They are invited to explore the Christian way of life as it is mediated through the Ignatian/Jesuit tradition. From this perspective, students wrestle with the implications of the message of Jesus in the areas of justice, personal integrity, sexuality, and life issues. Students explore these ethical issues through the reading of various documents from the Church's magisterium and other assigned readings, projects, and case studies. Through the course, students are invited to grow in awareness of self and others, both conceptually and effectively. To augment this development, students work in a variety of contexts—lecture, small/large group discussions (coed and single gender), and a required day–long junior retreat.

Course Outcomes:

By the end of this course, students will be able to:

1. Use the tools and language of moral reasoning to address moral questions relating to personal integrity, sexuality, social justice, and life issues.
2. Use research and analysis skills to synthesize information and insight from a variety of sources, including Scripture, Catholic tradition, and natural law for moral reflection.
3. Articulate the connection between moral reasoning and related information or insight from psychology, literature, art, science, etc.
4. Use the skills of dialogue and conflict resolution to work cooperatively with others to frame moral questions and engage in moral decision–making.
5. Identify the moral questions or frame the moral problems when presented with a situation or event in its context (whether that context is a factual news report, a personal experience, or a fictional work of literature or film).
6. Identify the persons affected by a moral decision, the full range of response options and resources available to a moral agent, the critical elements of context or history, and any information missing or needed to make a better moral decision.
7. Express the role of prayer in the moral process, after experiencing a variety of prayer forms.
8. Articulate a personal process for making moral choices that involves the mind, the heart, the spirit and the body, and apply to concrete situations.

Major Course Assessments:

1. Written tests on concepts and terminology.
2. Personal integration reflection papers.
3. Moral issue analysis papers.
4. Group projects in moral reasoning and analysis.
5. Non–verbal performance or product raising and/or responding to a moral issue.

Major Resources/Texts:

Units/Content Blocks:

(Note: For each unit/content block, the Religious Studies Department will develop outcomes, assessments, and suggested strategies over the next couple of years, and will revise these as necessary in an on–going way.)

1. Conscience
2. Human person as moral agent
3. Theological/sacramental process of conversion
4. Foundations of moral reasoning
5. Moral authority: the communal/ecclesial dimension of ethics
6. Moral decision–making steps
7. Applied ethics: justice issues
8. Applied ethics: personal integrity
9. Applied ethics: sexuality
10. Applied ethics: life issues
11. Moral imagination of the artist

Loyola Academy, Willmette, Illinois

Figure 7.14

Preschool/Kindergarten Interdisciplinary Unit: Japan

I. Outcome: Children will demonstrate knowledge of Japan's geographical form and topography.

Assessment: Children construct an edible island showing the geography and topography of Japan.

Suggested Strategies:
- large group discussion of land formation
- display large pictures of Japanese landscape
- present large scale island model
- children ask questions about pictures and model

II. Outcome: Children will display global awareness and demonstrate appreciation for Japanese food and style of eating.

Assessment: Children help plan, prepare and eat a Japanese meal using appropriate Japanese manners and customs.

Suggested Strategies:
- practice manners
- make setting for meal
- cook meal
- eat meal

III. Outcome: Children will apply knowledge of counting from 1–10 in Japanese.

Assessment: Children listen to Japanese folktale "Little Bunny and the Crocodile" and count in Japanese as numbers appear in the story.

Suggested Strategies:
- discuss concept of folktale
- teach counting 1–10 in Japanese
- provide posters with number 1–10, pronunciation key
- children hop across crocodile shapes on floor while counting

IV. Outcome: Children will participate in Japanese movement activity.

Assessment: Children create Japanese carp kites and use the kites in interpreting selected Japanese music.

Suggested Strategies:
- make kites
- learn children's day song
- learn dance/movement activity

V. Outcome: Children will experience the intricacies of an ancient Japanese art form.

Assessment: Children fold a simple origami animal.

Suggested Strategies:
- show and explain Japanese paper folding
- practice paper folding on plain paper before using origami paper for animal

Pam Hickey and Kim Feyen, Nativity School, Dubuque, Iowa

As with the format, no *one* process best suits every school. **Figure 7.15** outlines the essential steps for writing a curriculum that works. The obvious advantage of beginning with graduation outcomes and proceeding to subject area outcomes, grade level/cluster and course outcomes, and finally units is that the broader, more inclusive outcomes provide the basis for selecting and framing more specific outcomes. The disadvantage lies in the sometimes considerable time gap that occurs between formulating graduation outcomes and designing units that impact teaching.

In an elementary school, faculty might work together during year one to formulate graduation outcomes and then begin the rest of the process with one subject area. In the second, third and fourth years of the process, faculty would develop written curriculum for one to three additional subject areas, depending on the size of the school and the level of departmentalization in teaching assignments. In a high school, faculty might use year one to formulate graduation and department outcomes. In years two, three and four, departments would write course syllabi. The length of the process will depend on the size and expertise of the faculty, the number of courses offered, and additional resources available, such as diocesan or state outcomes, consultants, and the possibility of release time.

The writing process can move more quickly by assigning individuals or small teams different parts to draft and bring to the group for discussion and consensus. However, what a school gains in speed might be lost in the creativity and positive synergy that group decision-making can generate.

People with a fairly strong tolerance for ambiguity will find curriculum writing easier than folks who prefer logical sequences. The greatest point of impact of the curriculum with students lies in the units. **Figure 7.16** suggests four different "orders" in which to make unit decisions. All four can result in a statement of curriculum that connects outcomes, assessments and strategies. These statements can be framed into the selected format and then used by teachers to teach the curriculum. It does not matter which starting point teachers use, so long as the intended learning (concept, information, skill, generalization, value) becomes articulated as an outcome that serves as the basis for designing assessment and selecting strategies. Sometimes, visualizing a culminating performance task helps clarify the intended outcomes; sometimes, articulating the intended outcomes points to an authentic performance task. Considering appropriate criteria for evaluating

Figure 7.15

Steps for Writing Curriculum

1. Shift to an outcomes mindset
2. Articulate graduation outcomes.
   (Design culminating assessments.)
3. Articulate subject area outcomes.
4. Articulate grade/cluster level subject area and/or course level outcomes.
5. Design Units:
   - content
   - outcomes
   - assessments
   - strategies
   - resources
6. Monitor and coach.

Figure 7.16

Order of Planning

1. Identify "meaningful use tasks" related to subject matter.
2. Determine criteria for assessment of tasks.
3. Identify learnings embedded in tasks and assessment criteria; state as outcomes.
4. Suggest strategies.

Or
1. Identify desired/needed learnings; state as outcomes.
2. Construct performance tasks to assess learning.
3. Articulate standards for evaluating performance tasks.
4. Suggest needed strategies.

Or
1. Determine concepts, skills, generalizations to be included.
2. Translate into outcomes.
3. Design tasks/assessments.
4. Suggest strategies.

Or
1. Determine concepts, skills, generalizations to be included.
2. Design performance tasks/criteria for assessment to demonstrate concepts, skills, generalization .
3. Articulate as outcomes.
4. Suggest likely strategies.

performances may further clarify embedded outcomes; clearly stated outcomes may indicate evaluation criteria and so on. **Whatever the "order of planning," however, teachers should use the output model decision-making flow to *verify* results.** In other words, in the proposed curriculum: 1) Are the outcomes significant and clearly stated? 2) Do the assessments *match* the outcomes? 3) Will the strategies likely promote achievement of the outcomes as demonstrated in the assessments?

Neither outcomes alone nor assessments alone make a curriculum that works. A string of assessment tasks that is not grounded in clearly identified learning outcomes has less power to connect to other learning. Learning outcomes for which no assessment tasks have been identified do not provide enough framework for the instructional decisions that teachers make in a curriculum that works. Together, both point to strategies that teachers can help each other use to increase the desired learning. The total impact of the educational program at a school is severely lessened when all these decisions need to be made by each teacher individually each time he plans a unit. A written curriculum that connects outcomes, assessments and strategies in the way described in this book serves as a key tool for increasing the impact and effectiveness of the educational program across grades, courses and teachers.

Figure 7.17 outlines a series of suggested inservices to prepare a faculty to develop an outcomes-centered written curriculum. One approach might be to engage the faculty in appropriate inservice together during the school year and then to use available funding to hire groups of teachers to do draft writing in the summer. Teachers could then teach the draft curriculum during the next school year and make necessary revisions while creating the next draft.

The process may seem unending and interminable as you read this. But keep in mind that as the faculty's mindset changes and work progresses in one area, teachers will find themselves going about their instructional planning differently in other areas that might not be part of the "official" work in progress. The positive impact on learning and teaching of adopting an outcomes-centered approach will out pace the written results. Persisting through the completion of a written curriculum for the total educational program will then lay the foundation for an ongoing, meaningful and relatively painless curriculum review and revision process (which is unending in effective schools).

Figure 7.17

Suggested Faculty Inservice Series
Creating a Curriculum That Works

Overall Outcomes:
1. Clarify an effective approach to curriculum development that supports school's goals.
2. Determine format for development of written curriculum.
3. Design curriculum development process for faculty.
4. Establish action plan and timeline.

Session I:* Defining a Curriculum That Works
- What is outcomes-centered curriculum?
- Why is it so effective?
- How does it differ from curriculum based on goals and objectives?
- What does it look like on paper?

Outcomes:

Participants will:
- Explain the key components of outcomes-centered curriculum and connect it to school's goals.
- Examine examples of written curriculum.

Activities/Assessments:
1. "Think-pair-share" exercise about key components of outcomes-centered curriculum and its relation to school goals.
2. Whip-around personal reaction to sample curriculum; rank order formats.

Assignment:

Please prepare for Session II by completing the following:
I. Compare current course outlines/syllabi in your school with samples from Session I.
- What would it take to make your written curriculum more closely aligned with the samples?
- Do you think it could work? Would it make your course/ grade level outlines more effective in helping teachers increase learning?
- Is there some other way to make connections among   outcomes, assessments and strategies that would work better in your teaching? (Be ready to share your model.)
II. Bring one of your current course/unit outlines on overhead transparencies.

Session II: Writing a Curriculum Teachers Can Use to Increase Learning
1. What are the essential components of a written curriculum that helps teachers build a match among learning outcomes, assessments and strategies?
2. What will work at this school?
3. How do assessments factor into curriculum development in a critical way?

Outcomes:

Participants will:
- Explain the key components of outcomes-centered curriculum and connect it to school's goals.

---

* Some sessions will require more than one meeting, if time is limited to an hour or two for each session.

continued on next page

Figure 7.17 continued

- Share and discuss models of written curriculum that support a match among outcomes, assessments and strategies.
- Select a possible format for development of a written curriculum at the school.
- Identify criteria for designing authentic assessments.

Activities/Assessments:

1. Present and discuss models. Describe how each model includes components of outcomes-centered curriculum and how each connects to school's goals.
2. Agree on most promising model.
3. List characteristics of authentic assessment.

Assignment:

Please prepare for Session III by responding to the following:

"Think of the knowledge to be tested as a tool for fashioning a performance or product. Successful task design requires making the essential material of the course a necessary means to a successful performance end." (Grant Wiggins)

Choose one subject/course you teach. What might be 8 to 10 important performance tasks that effectively and efficiently map   the essential content? Describe each in several sentences, indicating what students will do, what areas of knowledge will be required and what skills they will need.

Session III: Designing a Process for the School

- What should be included in an outcomes-centered written curriculum at this school?
- How can we achieve it?

Outcomes:

Participants will:

- Examine the place of performance assessments in outcomes-centered curriculum.
- Select a possible format for a written curriculum at the school.
- Outline a curriculum development process for faculty.
- Determine next steps.

Activities/Assessments:

1. Present examples of outcomes and matching authentic assessments.
2. Outline format for the school's written curriculum.
3. In cooperative groups, prepare action plans for developing the written curriculum.

Assignment:

To prepare for Session IV, please complete the following:

I. Identify and/or locate two or three key resources for updating current best thinking about teaching and learning in your subject area.
II. Arrange for the resources to be available to faculty for Session IV.

Session IV: Reviewing Current Research

(As with the other sessions, this might require more than one session; if curriculum will be written for several subject areas simultaneously, multiple

continued on next page

Figure 7.17 continued

input sessions would also take place simultaneously.)

- What are the standards for this subject area on the elementary/secondary level?
- What kinds of assessments are being developed to assess learning according to the standards?
- What kinds of technology are especially appropriate to significant learning in this area?
- Which teaching practices should be increasing and which should be decreasing in relation to new standards and research on effective learning?
- What priorities do the school's mission, philosophy and graduation outcomes establish for significant learning in this subject area?

Outcomes:

Participants will:

1. Examine latest standards for elementary/secondary education in the subject area.
2. Discuss current research on effective teaching practices related to the subject area and the standards.
3. Discuss implications/requirements placed on learning in this subject area by mission and philosophy.
4. Reach consensus on key beliefs about content, process, teaching, and learning in the subject area that will inform the curriculum at the school.

Consulting Others

Locally developed curriculum stands the only chance of being effective because it can take into account the needs, experiences, and resources of the local community. This does not mean that each school must create everything from scratch. Central offices, professional organizations, publishers, testing companies can all provide useful resources for identifying outcomes, assessments, and strategies. The local school however, must make the connections among outcomes, assessments and strategies at the point at which the written curriculum most directly impacts instruction: grade level/cluster, course and unit.

Figure 7.18 presents one example of the kind of framework a diocesan office can provide to assist schools in local curriculum development. The first page of the example lists twenty-three K-8 language arts outcomes. These outcomes were formulated by a committee of expert teachers and administrators, working with current research and state mandates. For each outcome (or in some cases, combination of outcomes), the committee developed a set of framework indicators for K-2, 3-5 and 6-8. These indicators function as grade level/cluster outcomes. In addition, the guide sheets include categories of appropriate assessments and suggested strategies.

Figure 7.18

Archdiocesan Valued Outcomes For Language Arts

- Reads for pleasure and information
- Sets purpose for reading, adjusts speed and method accordingly
- Recognizes purposes and styles of writing
- Interprets literal and inferred meaning
- Recognizes the most important information in any text
- Summarizes main idea in own words
- Reads critically for fact/opinion, bias and validity
- Defines unfamiliar words by decoding, context, or dictionary
- Applies specific reading strategies to comprehend reading material
- Writes using planning, drafting, and revising to communicate
- Selects, organizes and relates coherent paragraphs
- Uses Standard English in sentences in regards to: Structure, Form, Punctuation, Spelling
- Modifies writing style for different readers and purposes
- Gathers information from sources using quotes or paraphrasing
- Writes reports using technical information from sources
- Writes creatively in stories, poems, and essays
- Writes for specific purpose, such as persuasion or description
- Engages in constructive class discussions with peers and teacher
- Follows spoken instructions
- States main idea of spoken presentations, can summarize
- Listens critically to spoken presentations, and separates fact/opinion
- Prepares and delivers oral presentations clearly and correctly
- Communicates effectively one–on–one, interacting with all ages

KERA* Goal #1:   **Use basic communication and math skills for purposes and situations similar to what he/she will encounter in life.**

Basic Skill #2:   **Gathering information and ideas through reading, observing and listening.**

Archdiocesan Valued Outcome: Recognize different purposes and styles of Meanings.

Framework indicators:

By the end of K–2 the student will:

Assessment Recommendation

T – Read for a variety of purposes.
C – Respond in a variety of ways to what has been read.

By the end of Grades 3–5 the student will:

T – Read for a variety of purposes.
C – Respond in a variety of ways to what has been read.
C – Recognize figurative techniques: imagery, simile
   – Relate one literary work to another.

By the end of Grades 6–8 the student will:

T – Read for a variety of purposes.
C – Respond in a variety of ways to what has been read.

*KERA is the Kentucky Education Reform Act

continued on next page

Figure 7.18 continued

C – Recognize figurative techniques: (onomatopeia, hyperbole, exaggeration).
P – Relate one literary work to another.
C – Recognize a variety of writing styles: testimonials, bandwagon, transfer, flashback, foreshadowing, propaganda.

Assessments:

Criterion Referenced Test	Performance Assessment	Teacher Checklist
Teacher–made test	PTS conferences	Teacher observations
Diocesan standardized test	Anecdotal records	Anecdotal records
Commerical standardized test	Student presentations	

Suggested Learning Strategies:

Teacher Directed	Cooperative	Independent
Word study	Word study	Word study
Compare & contrast	Compare & contrast	Compare & contrast
Group discussion	Reports	Reports
Plays	Book reports	Free response essays
Poetry readings	Group discussion	Poetry readings
Small group instruction	Plays	Student presentations
Guided reading	Poetry readings	Research reports
	Peer tutoring	

Assessment Recommendation (Key)

T = Teacher Checklist
C = Criterion Referenced Test
P = Performance Assessment Task

KERA Goal #1:   Use Basic communication and math skills for purposes and situations similar to what he/she will encounter in life.

Basic Skill #1:   Accessing information and ideas

Archdiocesan Valued Outcomes: • Gathers information from sources using quotes or paraphrasing.
• Writes reports using technical information from sources

Framework Indicators:

By the end of K–2 the student will:

Assessment Recommendation

P – Use library skills to locate selections of personal interest
P – Develop questioning techniques to clarify meaning and gain additional information
P/T – Explore ideas with one another in groups or pairs
P/T – Copy quotes and information to support ideas in a report

By the end of Grades 3–5 the student will:

P – Utilize interview techniques to obtain information from resource people
C/P – Demonstrate the effective use of reference tools

continued on next page

Figure 7.18 continued

By the end of 6–8 the student will:

P   – Utilize interview techniques to obtain information from resource people
P/T – Demonstrate the effective use of reference tools

Assessments:

Criterion Referenced Test	Performance Assessment	Independent
Teacher–made test	Student-generated products	Teacher observation
Diocesan standardized test	Bibliography preparation	Library skills checklist
Commercial standardized test	Changing one form of literary work to another	
	Student–created test	

Suggested Learning Strategies:

Teacher Directed	Cooperative	Independent
Discussions	Discussions	Note taking
Presentations	Presentations	Visiting libraries
Guided study of research/ various fields	Study of research/ various fields	Database
Interviews	Modems	Word processing
Team planning	Networking	
Publications	Publications	
Peer editing/revision		

Assessment Recommendation (Key)

T = Teacher Checklist
C = Criterion Referenced Test
P = Performance Assessment Task

KERA Goal #1:   Use Basic communication and math skills for purposes and situations similar to what he/she will encounter in life.

Basic Skill #4:   Expressing information, ideas, and emotions through writing.
Archdiocesan valued outcome: Writes creatively in stories, poems and essays.

Framework Indicators:

By the end of K–2 the student will:
Assessment Recommendation

P – Dictate a story about real life activities or feelings
P – Express descriptions of characters and setting

By the end of Grades 3–5 the student will:

C/P – Choose words which create a consistent mood and arouse the reader's interest
P – Write a social letter using standard form and practice
P – Use description to present characters and setting

By the end of Grades 6–8 the student will:

C/P – Choose words which create a consistent mood and arouse the reader's interest
P – Write a social letter using standard form and practice
P – Use description to present characters and setting
P – Write persuasive articles, essays or letters to convince the reader

continued on next page

Figure 7.18 continued

Assessments:

Criterion Referenced Test	Performance Assessment	Independent
Teacher–made test	Student presentation	Teacher observation
Diocesan standardized test	PTS conference	Literary analysis
Commercial standardized test	Student written work	
Anecdotal records		

Suggested Learning Strategies:

Teacher Directed	Cooperative	Independent
Editing	Discussions	Poetry reading
Discussions	Plays	Categorizing ideas
Plays	Poetry reading	Literary analysis
Literary analysis	Peer editing	Compare/contrast
	Categorizing ideas	
	Author circles	
	Literary analysis	
	Publications	
	Team support	

Assessment Recommendation (Key)

  T = Teacher Checklist
  C = Criterion Referenced Test
  P = Performance Assessment Task

Archdiocese of Louisville, 1991

These materials do not constitute a written curriculum for a school because they are not specific enough to indicate the intended connections among outcomes, assessments and strategies at the grade level/cluster, course and unit levels. However, a resource like this provides tremendous help to schools in developing their curriculum. Formulating graduation level subject area outcomes and grade/cluster level outcomes at the diocesan level allows schools to use the expertise of teachers who are especially well trained and current in a given subject area. The work of the central committee then serves as a *context* within which schools can develop local curriculum. Moreover, when the school develops curriculum consistent with diocesan outcomes and framework indicators, the school can rest assured that all important learnings and current thinking about best practices have been included. At the same time, the school maintains its responsibility for specifying the connections among more specific instructional decisions that will constitute its own curriculum. The availability of these kinds of diocesan resources will also significantly reduce the time it takes a school to develop its written curriculum.

Figure 7.19 offers another form of appropriate diocesan assistance. In this example, the expert committee formulated specific grade level outcomes related to the NCTM program level outcomes (K-4) and the general scope and sequence for mathematics being used by most schools. Working from the grade level outcomes, individual schools would develop their own written curriculum that connects outcomes, assessments and strategies for the grade level and for units within the grade level. Although specifying *individual* grade level outcomes gives local curriculum committees more detailed examples of grade-appropriate outcomes to work with in developing their own curriculum, it also locks them into more detailed scope and sequence. Specifying *cluster* grade level outcomes (**Figure 7.18**) allows for greater diversity in scope and sequence among schools while still providing samples from which to individualize. If a diocesan-wide testing program exists, greater consistency in scope and sequence of learning in a subject area may be important.

High schools can also benefit from diocesan-level expert committees that formulate subject area outcomes and develop model assessments that reflect current research and best practice. These outcomes and sample assessments then function as parameters within which course syllabi and units are developed and against which they are screened. On both the grade school and high school levels, we must remember that subject-area outcomes formulated at the diocesan level will need to be adapted by the individual school in light of its unique set of values stated in the mission, philosophy and graduation outcomes.

Finally, **Figures 10.4** and **10.13** in Chapter Ten offer another format for central office assistance in local curriculum development. In this case, a multi-diocese task force developed a set of K-12 Religious Education Outcomes. The guide sheet for each outcome includes subcategories of learning and sample assessments at grades 3, 8 and 12. Again, these outcomes and guide sheets do not constitute a written curriculum for a school; they provide a useful, current, and comprehensive context within which local educators can create a curriculum that works for their students.

Summing It Up

Developing a written curriculum that helps teachers increase learning for all students across grades and over time cannot be reduced to a step-by-step formula. We can clearly identify the essential components of such a curriculum. We can examine various samples of written curriculum that include the essential components and respect the principles of outcomes-centered decision-making. We can identify appropriate assistance from diocesan offices. In the end, local educators must use these tools to create a common mindset that will inform their choices about format, content, and process.

Figure 7.19

Elementary Mathematics
(Partial Sample)

The attached sample suggests:

1) Subject area goals for mathematics, based on NCTM Standards.

2) Program level outcomes (K–4) for six areas, taken from the Office of Catholic Education Math Module (Chicago) using outcomes derived from the NCTM Standards.

3) Grade level outcomes for grades K, 1, 2, 3 and 4 relating to the six areas identified in the K–4 program level outcomes: problem solving, communication, reasoning, connections, measurement and probability and statistics.

Mathematical Goals

The Math Curriculum has, as a central aim, to develop in students the mathematical "power" needed for today's society. Toward this end, the K–8 curriculum articulates six goals essential to all students that they:

- Learn to communicate mathematically
- Become mathematical problem solvers
- Become confident in their own ability to think mathematically
- Learn to value mathematics
- Learn to reason mathematically
- Appreciate the connection between math and all subject areas

Curriculum and Evaluation Standards For School Mathematics National Council of Teachers of Mathematics

Program Level Outcomes Grades K—4

Standard 1: Mathematics as Problem Solving

In grades K–4, the study of mathematics should emphasize problem solving so that students can

- use problem–solving approaches to investigate and understand mathematical content;
- formulate problems from everyday

and mathematical situations;
- develop and apply strategies to solve a wide variety of problems;
- verify and interpret results with respect to the original problem;
- acquire confidence in using mathematics meaningfully.

Standard 2: Mathematics as Communication

In grades 1–4, the study of mathematics should include numerous opportunities for communication so that students can

- relate physical materials, pictures and diagrams to mathematical ideas;
- reflect on and clarify their thinking about mathematical ideas and situations.
- relate their everyday language to mathematical language and symbols;
- realize that representing, discussing, reading, writing and listening to mathematics are a vital part of learning and using mathematics.

Standard 3: Mathematics as Reasoning

In grades K–4, the study of mathematics should emphasize reasoning so that students can

- draw logical conclusions about mathematics;
- use models, known facts, properties and relationships to explain their thinking;
- justify their answers and solution processes;
- use patterns and relationships to analyze mathematical situations;
- believe that mathematics makes sense.

Standard 4: Mathematical Connections

In grades K–4, the study of mathematics should include opportunities to make

continued on next page

Figure 7.19 continued

connections so that students can

- link conceptual and procedural knowledge;
- relate various representations of concepts or procedures to one another;
- recognize relationships among different topics in mathematics;
- use mathematics in other curriculum areas;
- use mathematics in their daily lives.

Standard 10: Measurement

In grades K–4, the mathematics curriculum should include measurement so that students can

- understand the attributes of length, capacity, weight, area, volume, time, temperature and angle;
- develop the process of measuring and concepts related to units of measurement;
- make and use estimates of measurement;
- make and use measurements in problem and everyday situations.

Standard 11: Statistics and Probability

In grades K–4, the mathematics curriculum should include experiences with data analysis and probability so that students can

- collect, organize and describe data;
- construct, read, and interpret displays of data;
- formulate and solve problems that involve collecting and analyzing data;
- explore concepts of chance.

Grade Level Outcomes

Kindergarten

1. **Problem Solving**
   a. Act out a story.
   b. Use manipulatives to solve problems.
   c. Use color coding.
2. **Communication**
   a. Talk about sets of objects, numbers and shapes.
3. **Reasoning**
   a. Talk about sets of objects, numbers and shapes.
   b. Identify, duplicate and create patterns.
   c. Group objects according to common attributes.
4. **Connections**
   a. Recognize and develop the mathematical situations occurring in children's literature.
   b. Recognize and develop the mathematical situations occurring in science.
10. **Measurement**
   a. Use manipulatives to determine lengths of objects.
   b. Compare two objects by specified attributes such as length, weight, volume and temperature.
11. **Probability and Statistics**
   a. Collect and organize objects and information
   b. Construct and interpret real graphs.

Grade I

1. **Problem Solving**
   a. Formulate problems from everyday and mathematical situations.
   b. Act out a story problem.
   c. Retell and/or illustrate a story problem.
   d. Use manipulatives to solve problems.
   e. Verify results with respect to the original problem.
   f. Investigate new mathematical situations using previously learned knowledge.
2. **Communication**
   a. Talk about relationships between sets of objects and numbers.
   b. Draw pictures or use objects to illustrate an understanding of the mathematical topics studied.

continued on next page

Figure 7.19 continued

c. Write about mathematics topics presented at this level.

3. **Reasoning**
   a. Identify similar objects according to common attributes.
   b. Use skip counting to complete a number pattern.
   c. Verify an answer to a problem.

4. **Connections**
   a. Recognize and develop the relationship between measurement and the number line.
   b. Recognize and develop the mathematical situations occurring in children's literature.
   c. Recognize and develop mathematical applications in social studies, such as graphs, tables and map skills.
   d. Recognize and develop the use of mathematical skills and concepts in science, such as measurement, graphs and data analysis.
   e. Recognize and develop the use of shapes in art.
   f. Recognize and develop the use of rhythm patterns in music.

10. **Measurement**
    a. Use nonstandard units to measure length, area, weight and volume.
    b. Demonstrate the need for a uniform unit of length.
    c. Identify and give the value of pennies, nickels and dimes.
    d. Measure and estimate length to the nearest centimeter and inch.
    e. Identify the given time on a clock using hours and half–hours.
    f. Identify days of the week.
    g. Discuss terminology related to temperature, weight and length.

11. **Probability and Statistics**
    a. Collect and organize information.
    b. Construct and interpret real and picture graphs.
    c. Determine which is most likely to happen from give information.

Grade 2
1. **Problem Solving**

a. Formulate problems from everyday and mathematical situations.
b. Solve problems that require the use of strategies such as making a list, drawing a picture, looking for a pattern, etc.
c. Use manipulatives to solve problems.
d. Verify results with respect to the original problem.
e. Investigate new mathematical situations using previously learned knowledge.

2. **Communication**
   a. Discuss mathematical concepts and relationships.
   b. Draw pictures and use objects to illustrate mathematical concepts.
   c. Write about mathematics topics presented at this level.

3. **Reasoning**
   a. Use addition to complete a number pattern.
   b. Identify and describe what comes next in a pictorial pattern.
   c. Verify an answer to a problem.

4. **Connections**
   a. Recognize and develop the relationship between addition and subtraction.
   b. Recognize and develop the mathematical situations occurring in children's literature.
   c. Recognize and develop mathematical applications in social studies, such as graphs, tables and map skills.
   d. Recognize and develop the use of mathematical skills and concepts in science, such as measurement, graphs and data analysis.
   e. Recognize and develop the use of geometry in nature, art and architecture.
   f. Recognize and develop the use of probability and statistics to describe and predict events that occur in nature.

continued on next page

Figure 7.19 continued

g. Recognize and develop the use of money.

10. Measurement

a. Read a thermometer calibrated using the Fahrenheit and Celsius scales.

b. Estimate and use nonstandard units to measure area.

c. Estimate weight using nonstandard units.

d. Demonstrate the need for a uniform unit of weight.

e. Estimate capacity using cups and pints.

f. Describe the relationship of inch, foot, and yard.

g. Describe the relationship of centimeter and meter.

h. Measure to the nearest inch, centimeter, foot, yard, or meter.

i. Recognize the time represented by succeeding numerals on a clock as a five minute interval.

j. Identify the value of quarters, half–dollars and dollars.

k. Identify the value of a collection of pennies, nickels, dimes, and quarters whose total value is less than a dollar.

11. Probability and Statistics

a. Collect data, construct, and interpret picture and bar graphs.

b. Write a story problem using information from a graph.

c. Determine which event is most likely or least likely to happen given appropriate information.

Grade 3

1. Problem Solving

a. Formulate problems from everyday and mathematical situations.

b. Choose the appropriate operation in simple word problems and multiple step problems through use of pictures and diagrams, tables, graphs, example, and cooperative learning.

c. Select and use concrete materials and manipulatives to assist in problem solving.

d. Use computer software programs to assist in problem solving.

e. Verify results with respect to the original problem.

f. Investigate new mathematical situations using previously learned knowledge.

2. Communication

a. Discuss mathematical concepts and relationships.

b. Draw pictures and use objects to illustrate mathematical concepts.

c. Write about mathematics topics presented at this level.

3. Reasoning

a. Use addition or subtraction to continue a number pattern.

b. Identify the missing information needed to find a solution to a given story problem.

c. Compare and contrast geometric figures.

d. Verify an answer to a problem.

4. Connections

a. Recognize and develop the relationship between addition and multiplication.

b. Recognize and develop the relationship between fractions and decimals.

c. Recognize and develop the mathematical situations occurring in children's literature.

d. Recognize and develop mathematical applications in social studies, such as graphs, tables, and map skills.

e. Recognize and develop the use of mathematical skills and concepts in science, such as measurement, graphs and data analysis.

f. Recognize and develop the use of geometry in nature, art, and architecture.

10. Measurement

a. Tell time to the nearest minute.

continued on next page

Figure 7.19 continued

b. Measure line segments to the nearest half–inch and quarter–inch.

c. Investigate perimeters.

d. Add units of length that may or may not require regrouping of inches to feet or centimeters to meters.

e. Estimate weight using pounds and kilograms.

f. Estimate capacity using quarts, gallons, and liters.

g. Given a standard unit, estimate and measure the area of a rectangular region.

h. Given a standard unit, estimate the area of any region.

i. Investigate the addition of hour and half–hour time intervals.

j. Identify the value of any collection of coins and dollars.

k. Given an amount of money, determine if a purchase can be made.

11. Probability and Statistics

a. Collect data, construct, and interpret picture and bar graphs.

b. Interpret circle graphs.

c. Write a story problem using information from a graph.

d. Given appropriate information, determine which is most likely or least likely to happen or whether one event is more likely than another.

Grade 4

1. Problem Solving

a. Formulate problems from everyday situations.

b. Draw a picture to solve a problem.

c. Utilize patterns in problem solving.

d. Utilize map information in problem solving.

e. Make diagrams to solve problems.

f. Use outside sources such as an Infobank.

g. Verify results.

h. Investigate new mathematical situations using previously learned knowledge.

2. Communication

a. Discuss mathematical concepts and relationships.

b. Draw pictures or diagrams to illustrate mathematical concepts.

c. Use manipulatives to illustrate mathematical concepts.

d. Write word problems about real life situations and discuss.

3. Reasoning

a. Use addition or subtraction or multiplication to continue a number pattern.

b. Analyze statements that use "and", "or", or "not."

c. Determine number of ways an event can occur.

d. Verify an answer to a problem.

4. Connections

a. Recognize and develop the relationship between addition and multiplication.

b. Recognize and develop the relationship between fractions and decimals.

c. Recognize and develop the relationship between measurement and fractions.

d. Recognize and develop mathematical skills and concepts in science, such as measurement and graphs.

e. Recognize and develop mathematical applications in social studies, such as graphs, tables, and map skills.

f. Recognize and develop the use of money and banking applications.

g. Recognize and develop the use of probability and statistics to describe and predict events that occur in nature.

10. Measurement

a. Subtract unit of length that may not require renaming of feet to inches or meters to centimeters.

continued on next page

Figure 7.19 continued

b. Select an appropriate unit of measure for a given situation.

c. Investigate the addition of minutes to a specified time.

d. Determine the amount of change to be received form a purchase.

e. Measure right angles, acute angles, obtuse angles, and straight angles.

11. Probability and Statistics

a. Collect data, construct, and interpret picture, bar, circle, and line graphs.

b. Write a story problem using information from a graph.

c. Investigate the probability of an event occurring.

Chapter Eight:

 **Designing Valid Assessments**

Principle 6: Outcomes and assessments *together* form the basis of a curriculum *that works*.

A good set of learning outcomes provides the strongest foundation possible for building a curriculum that works, but outcomes alone are not enough. Outcomes are observed and assessed in specific tasks and situations, in performances. A performance can be an essay, a speech, a constructed model, a mathematical proof, a dance, a play, a debate, an experiment, a journal, a painting, a fitness routine, a conversation in French, a prayer service, or any other opportunity for a student to use knowledge and skills to create an answer or product. Students can do performances individually or together. They can do them in one day or one week or one semester. These performances specify the outcomes for this student or group of students in this instructional period.

Performances are the way we assess achievement of the outcomes. A performance will be both more specific and more inclusive of other learnings than the particular outcome it assesses. It will be more connected to a concrete, real-life situation, more creative, and more individualized. In designing the performances we will use to assess outcomes at appropriate points in the curriculum, and in establishing assessment categories and criteria, scoring scales, and rubrics for assessing those performances, we determine the sequence and scope of the curriculum in pursuit of the outcomes.

Learning means responding more and more effectively to the situation. *Responding* implies action and requires knowledge, skills, motivation, and conviction. *Effectively* has to do with goals and values. A real situation is always multidimensional, multimodal, and connected. From what we know of how the brain works, learning is *necessarily* active, experiential, purposeful. In a curriculum that works, valid assessment of learning must assume the same characteristics.

When my daughter was in fifth grade, she consistently received grades of 3+ and 4 on a 4.0 scale in language arts, as measured on worksheets and tests involving matching, fill in the blank, and sample sentences. When asked by her leader to fill in an application for a Girl Scout project, she produced a document with multiple spelling errors, incomplete sentences, and numerous punctuation mistakes. Clearly, her school performance indicated mastery of isolated skills that did not transfer readily to real-life situations.

The language arts curriculum for the school could well have looked like those in **Figures 8.1** and **8.2**. Some of the statements in these examples appear in outcomes/objectives form, but as a string of isolated bits of knowledge and discrete skills. My daughter had learned something in language arts. She had learned to respond effectively to the situation, but the situation was completing worksheets and objective tests rather than using language mechanics to communicate real information.

Contrast this with a ninth grade English program which has as one of its outcomes, "Write a five paragraph expository paper, using a thesis statement and supporting evidence, in correct standard English." By the end of the year, virtually every freshman can do this to an acceptable standard of proficiency—in English class. Better than correct usage apart from actual writing, but what about transfer of skills to science reports? religion essays? social studies papers? What would it take to build a curriculum that coaches students to clear expository writing (report writing for most of us in our jobs) in all subject areas?

We would begin with the outcome stated above and then determine what student achievement of this outcome would look like—in English, in science, in social studies, in mathematics, and so on. To do this effectively, we would 1) design some concrete expository writing performance tasks in the various subject areas, 2) identify assessment categories (clarity of thesis, appropriateness of supporting evidence, effective use of language, etc.) in

Figure 8.1

Grammar and Usage
Program Goal

Program Objectives:

A. Defines and recognizes nouns
B. Defines and recognizes verbs
C. Defines and recognizes adjectives
D. Defines and recognizes adverbs
E. Defines and recognizes pronouns
F. Defines and recognizes prepositions, conjunctions, and interjections
G. Identifies and writes the basic sentence patterns

Subject Objectives:

		K	1	2	3	4	5	6	7	8
A.	**Nouns**									
A1.	Defines and recognizes nouns		Id	R	R	R	M			
A2.	Identifies singular, plural, common and proper nouns			I	Id	R	M			
A3.	Recognizes person, number and gender						Id			
A4.	Recognizes nominative, objective and possessive cases							Id	R	M
A5.	Identifies use of nouns as subject, object and indirect object					I	Id	R	M	
A6.	Identifies noun as object of preposition and direct object						I	R	M	
A7.	Identifies noun as an appositive and predicate noun						Id	R	R	M
A8.	Memorizes and uses rules for forming plurals of nouns			I	Id	R	R	R	M	
A9.	Recognizes irregular plural nouns				Id	R	R	R	M	
B.	**Verbs**									
B1.	Defines and recognizes verbs		I	I	Id	R	R	R	M	
B2.	Identifies principal parts of verbs				I	Id	R	R	M	
B3.	Distinguishes between principal/ helping verbs									
B4.	Distinguishes between transitive/ intransitive verbs									
B5.	Distinguishes between active/ passive verbs						I	Id	R	M
B6.	Identifies present, past and future tense				I	Id	R	R	M	
B7.	Identifies perfect tense						I	Id	R	M
B8.	Identifies active/passive voice						I	Id	R	M

R-Reinforce	Id-Identify
I-Introduce	M-Master

Figure 8.2

Grammar Skills

The learner applies knowledge of grammar skills in writing and
speaking.

Program Objectives:

A. Identifies and recognizes parts of speech

B. Recognizes components of sentence structure

C. Demonstrates ability to apply proper mechanics in written expression.

Sentence Structure	K	1	2	3	4	5	6	7	8
B1. Distinguishes elements of sentence structure:									
a. Word order in sentences	R	I	D	D	D	D	D	D	D
b. Complete subject		R	I	D	D	D	D	D	D
c. Complete predicate		R	I	D	D	D	D	D	D
d. Simple subject and simple predicate		R	I	D	D	D	D	*	*
e. Compound subject and compound predicate			R	I	D	D	D	D	D
f. Subject complements					I	D	D	D	D
g. Direct and indirect objects					I	D	D	D	D
h. Subject and verb agreement				I	D	D	D	D	D
B2. Recognizes sentence types:									
a. Declarative	R	I	D	D	D	D	D	*	*
b. Interrogative	R	I	D	D	D	D	D	*	*
c. Exclamatory	R	I	D	D	D	D	D	*	*
d. Imperative			I	D	D	D	D	*	*
B3. Identifies clauses and phrases:									
a. Prepositional phrases						I	D	D	D
b. Independent clauses								R	I
c. Noun, adjective, adverb clauses								R	I
d. Subordinate clauses								R	I
e. Participal, gerund, infinitive phrases							R	I	

R-Recognize　　I-Identify
D-Demonstrate

which to assess the writing performances, and 3) formulate a scoring scale and rubric for each assessment category. Eventually, we would develop a set of sample papers representing achievement at various levels of performance matching the scale, so that students and teachers have a clear, common vision of performance expectations.

The next step involves providing students with opportunity to write, receive feedback, write again. In other words, curriculum development in various subject areas would include designing performance assessments that involve expository writing and teachers using the assessment categories and rubrics to evaluate the students' work. In this example, the English department curriculum would probably include course and unit outcomes, assessments and strategies designed to *directly* coach the knowledge and skills needed by students to perform well in the assessment categories connected to the broad outcome. Curriculum in other subject areas would build on the direct instruction in English by using writing (assessed on the same categories and according to the same scoring scale and rubric) as one vehicle for students to demonstrate learning in the subject area.

The particular assessments involving expository writing will, of course, include more learning than the single outcome. A specific task might require accessing information, drawing inferences, creating scenarios, reaching an audience, explaining the solution to a problem, or presenting an original idea. In some of these instances, the assessment of the *writing* itself takes precedence; in some instances, the assessment of the writing assumes the status of *one* category among many others (accuracy of information, originality of design, etc.).

The critical piece here rests with the *connection* between the stated learning outcome and specific performances that validly assess the outcome. The presence of the outcome justifies the selection of the assessments; the specific assessments activate the outcome in concrete instructional situations by identifying standards and pointing to strategies. **Both outcomes and assessments must be developed in tandem to create a curriculum that works and increases learning for all students.**

The connection between outcomes and assessments bears further scrutiny. Reconsider **Figure 7.6** (page 94), a sample curriculum for a unit in high school biology. Note, especially, the outcomes and assessments. Now suppose that we keep the same outcomes, but substitute a new set of assessments (**Figure 8.3**). What happens to learning and teaching? This second set of assessments emphasizes declarative knowledge almost exclusively, with perhaps some expansion of knowledge in essays or short answer questions.

Students demonstrate the learning stated in the outcomes, but at the very lowest level. A classroom experience consistent with these assessments could remain largely lecture and question/answer. **A different set of assessments will create a different set of learnings, even when working from the same outcomes.**

In the same way, consider the effect on teaching/learning of substituting the assessments in **Figure 7.4** (page 90) with those in **Figure 8.4.** The first set of assessments supports a whole language environment in which language arts skills are developed and assessed in the context of real communication and active learning. The second set of assessments implies a much more teacher-centered, artificial learning environment in which students develop isolated skills following a textbook sequence. Again, a different set of assessments will create a different set of learnings, even when working from the same outcomes.

Because of the way the brain works, learning is driven and defined by what some educators refer to as "meaningful use tasks", performances or products that require students to *make connections* between classroom learning and real life. In other words, the proof of the pudding lies in what students can do with knowledge and skills in specific, real situations that are of some importance not only in school but also in the world beyond. Creating a curriculum that works means inviting and coaching students to do a full range of these important tasks increasingly well. The broad statements of these behaviors (ways of responding to the situation) are the outcomes. The specific situations (tasks) in which the behaviors are observed are the performance assessments. Identifying the kinds of knowledge and skills that students must learn to complete the meaningful use tasks and

---

Figure 8.3

Biology

Assessments:

1. Quiz on parts and functions of respiratory system.
2. Short answer questions on effect of select respiratory disorders on breathing and gas exchange.
3. Narrative explanation of diagram showing how oxygen and carbon dioxide are transported in the blood.
4. Unit test on information, including true/false, labeling diagram, short answer, and essay on effect of various environmental factors on respiration.

identifying the expected levels of proficiency of performance of the tasks results in what we sometimes have referred to as scope and sequence.

In this schema, *outcomes* may repeat throughout a K-12 curriculum (e.g., use technology to produce and communicate knowledge - graduation outcome). Specific *assessment tasks* will fit the level of the student and the subject matter (e.g., use word processing to write a story about you and your best friend—4th grade religion unit assessment). *Assessment categories* (areas of knowledge and skill to be assessed within the performance, indicating achievement of the learning stated in the outcome) will repeat to some extent (see framework indicators in **Figure 7.18** on page 116), but will also fit the level and experience of students, as will the scoring rubric.

A great deal of thought and collaboration must go into the process of selecting assessment tasks to fit the outcomes, setting scoring criteria, and ensuring reliable scoring. It is beyond the scope of this book to provide a detailed study of assessments—kinds, construction, scoring, use. Some excellent resources are listed in the resource section at the end of the chapter.

However, I do want to underline the close and critical connection between outcomes and assessments in creating a curriculum that works, and highlight the decision-making process that supports it. In talking about performance assessment, Grant Wiggins makes the following statement:

> Think of the knowledge to be tested as a tool for fashioning a performance or product. Successful task design requires making the essential material of a course a *necessary means* to a successful performance *end*.

Wiggins would agree that the statement presupposes learning outcomes. Using the frame of reference in this book for creating a curriculum that works, the thinking goes like this: "What should someone who has mastered this subject matter to a certain level of proficiency be able to do?" Operating within a mix of key concepts, generalizations, skills and information, what are eight to ten dynamic, authentic, real-life tasks that pro-

---

Figure 8.4
Language Arts: Writing

Assessments:
1. Grammar exercises.
2. Punctuation exercises:
3. Editing for mechanics quizzes.
4. Weekly paragraph following, write, edit, rewrite, process.

vide opportunity to demonstrate the essential learning? Outcomes point to assessments; assessments actualize outcomes.

Let me use a course I recently taught to illustrate how outcomes and assessments interact in the development of curriculum that works. The course was a graduate education course entitled, "Curriculum Direction in the Catholic High School." I began designing the course with this question: What should someone who is ready to exercise curriculum leadership in a high school be able to do at an entry level of expertise? The four answers comprised the outcomes for the course:

1. Articulate and use a process for developing/improving curriculum in a high school.

2. Use research and other sources appropriately to inform choices.

3. Connect teacher development, supervision and inservice to improving curriculum and instruction.

4. Use assessment and other forms of feedback to evaluate and revise curriculum and instruction.

Next, I asked myself, "What are 4 to 6 tasks (performances/concrete situations) that would give students opportunity to practice and receive feedback on these abilities, skills, areas of knowledge in situations that reflect real life?" The answers formed the core of assessments for the course:

1. Curriculum improvement plan

2. Syllabus critiques

3. Annotated bibliography and resource guide

4. Reflective response sheets on major theorists

5. Class discussion/participation

6. Job interview or curriculum committee agenda and simulated chairing of meeting.

If students could successfully complete these tasks, they would in fact demonstrate achievement of the learning indicated in the outcomes. For each assessment, I needed to establish and communicate assessment categories/criteria and scoring scales and rubrics. Class time and feedback on intermediate assignments allowed for modeling and coaching. Some of the assessments happened in teams; some were individual. The outline of classes specified content, skills, teaching/learning activities, feedback, and assignments in a progression that prepared students for the performance tasks as they came along.

The written curriculum for this course includes the overall course outcomes, the six integrative performance assessments and three units (curriculum design and development, implementation, and evaluation). For each unit the curriculum specifies content, outcomes, assessments/feedback, resources/materials, suggested strategies, and number of classes. The performance assessments comprise some of the unit assessments; other assessments provide feedback on acquisition and application of specific knowledge and skills needed for the performance assessments. The plans for individual classes are not part of the official curriculum; they belong to the teacher.

The six performance assessments working in tandem with the course outcomes result in a course that requires active, experiential, real-life learning from students. A course with the same outcomes, using information-based assessments alone, would likely not lead to the same active learning. In the same way, a course outline which identifies the "essential material" solely in terms of content (knowledge and understanding of) rather than as significant learning outcomes, would far more likely result in information-based testing and teacher lectures.

Not all assessments in a course (grade level/cluster) will be performance assessments. However, if learning is specified in outcomes and the outcomes are significant, then some of the assessments must be performance assessments to produce a curriculum that works.

The recently published ASCD book, *Teaching With the Dimensions of Learning*, presents a framework for instructional planning that takes into account five aspects of the learning process, including establishing a climate in which learning can best take place. In a context of clear expectations and feeling safe, students move to mastery and expertise by acquiring and integrating knowledge (declarative and procedural), by extending and refining the knowledge using critical thinking skills, and by using the knowledge and skills to engage in "meaningful use tasks." If students are also invited to reflect on their learning and practice self-assessment, they develop habits of mind that mark the life-long, self-regulated learning of effective adults and competent workers.

Using the approach to curriculum presented in this book, we could expect that curriculum for a unit would include outcomes and assessments that relate to all three phases of the learning process: the acquisition, extension, and use of knowledge. In other words, we would find outcomes that ask students to define and explain (acquisition), to compare, predict and generalize (extension), to produce products and create responses (meaningful use). *And* we would find assessment tasks that give students specific opportunities to demonstrate the learning in all these outcomes. The unit outcomes and the corresponding assessments are selected because they *enable* the significant learning indicated in the course outcomes and demonstrated in the integrative performance assessments for the course.

Not all outcomes are of equal dimension; not all assessments are authentic performance assessments. However, in a curriculum that works, the culminating outcomes for the course, subject area/cluster and graduation *will* be significant and the corresponding assessments *will* be authentic performances. Further, the decisions about what knowledge students acquire, how they extend and refine it and what they do with it are all made in direct relation to the significant, culminating outcomes and performance assessments.

Figures 8.5 and 8.6 attempt to diagram this approach to unit planning. Actual practice is not as neat and tidy or linear as the diagrams might suggest, but the overall conceptual flow stands pretty true. We design the units, of course, to enable achievement of the course/grade level/cluster outcomes and integrative assessments, which in turn enable achievement and demonstration of the discipline-specific and values-integrating outcomes which drive the curriculum.

Consider one final sketch of curriculum decision-making that makes effective use of the dynamic interaction of significant outcomes and authentic assessments. Motorola offers a summer technology camp for the children of its employees. The overall goal of the program is to have students learn about technology in the context of workplace use. Using the learnings needed for employees (**Figure 5.2**), components of the course include knowledge and skills, team experiences, authentic tasks, and feedback. Culminating outcome: To solve a complex problem, working as part of a team of junior engineers. The performance task for each team will specify the problem and involve teams in seeking input, planning together, working in hands-on ways, and explaining what they did (enabling outcomes). This camp has all the components of a curriculum that works: 1)

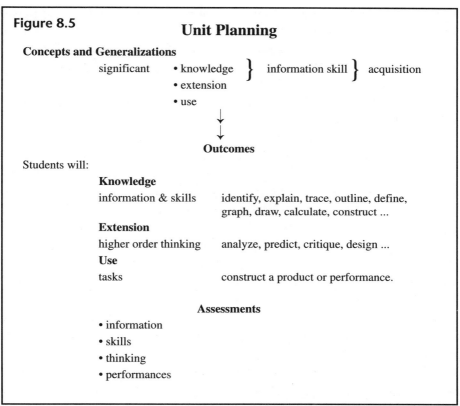

Figure 8.5

Unit Planning

Concepts and Generalizations

significant • knowledge } information skill } acquisition
• extension
• use

↓
↓

Outcomes

Students will:

Knowledge

information & skills identify, explain, trace, outline, define, graph, draw, calculate, construct ...

Extension

higher order thinking analyze, predict, critique, design ...

Use

tasks construct a product or performance.

Assessments

• information
• skills
• thinking
• performances

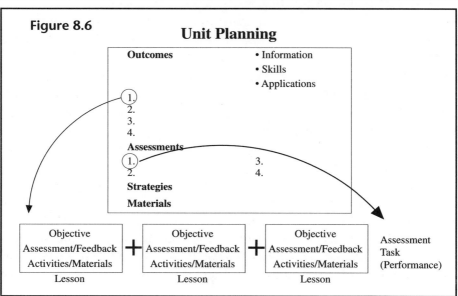

Figure 8.6

Unit Planning

Outcomes • Information
• Skills
• Applications

1.
2.
3.
4.

Assessments

1. 3.
2. 4.

Strategies

Materials

Objective Assessment/Feedback Activities/Materials	Objective Assessment/Feedback Activities/Materials	Objective Assessment/Feedback Activities/Materials	Assessment Task (Performance)
Lesson	Lesson	Lesson	

significant outcomes (central to the discipline and useful and needed in real life roles), 2) assessments that give students opportunity to demonstrate the learning in real contexts that require meaningful use of knowledge, skills, and motivation, and 3) strategies that cast the teacher in the role of coach and resource guide to active learners.

This kind of curriculum design should not be what only creative risk-taker teachers do; nor should it be available only to students with privileged eligibility based on test scores, tracks, or socio-economic status. Building a curriculum that works means looking at what we do in every classroom with the vision of the Motorola camp director. It means seeing what the learning is good for in the long run as well as the short run (significant outcomes). It means seeing integrative/culminating assessments as tasks, performances, rich and perhaps messy opportunities to concretely and creatively demonstrate the significant outcomes. It means seeing teaching as posing the task and then providing *all* children with the tools to accomplish it: content knowledge; technical, interpersonal and learning-to-learn skills; technology; motivation; feedback, feedback, feedback. In this kind of curriculum, simply averaging test scores over the year or semester makes little sense. It is the quality of the learning *after* enough coaching that counts. And "enough" is defined by the quality of the performance.

Outcomes and assessments work *together* to create a curriculum that works—that leads to more significant learning for more students. Outcomes identify the significant learning we are after; assessments provide the specific ways students demonstrate achievement of the learning identified in the outcomes. Three things make learning significant: 1) the learning is central to the subject area (not trivial); 2) the learning is useful beyond the classroom (connected to real life); 3) the learning is shaped by the integrating values of the school (graduation outcomes). Assessments that provide *valid* opportunities for students to demonstrate significant learning outcomes must go beyond paper and pencil, objective tests to include products and performances that require students to use knowledge, skills, and motivation in real-life contexts.

Not all assessments teachers use will involve these kinds of authentic performances. Teachers still need to evaluate and give students feedback on more "academic" learning outcomes (especially at lesson and unit levels). However, in a curriculum that works, it is essential that the more limited enabling outcomes and assessments **never** be the end-point or focus of the instructional process. Everything teachers do must be shaped by the exit outcomes (which represent significant learning) and by the matching authentic performances used to assess the exit/culminating outcomes.

Selected Resources

Herman, J.L., P.R. Aschbacher, L. Winters. (1992) *A Practical Guide to Alternative Assessment*. Alexandria, VA: Association for Supervision and Curriculum Development. (Includes references for more specific information for developing and using alternative assessments.)

Marzano, R.J. (1992) *A Different Kind of Classroom: Teaching with the Dimensions of Learning*. Alexandria, VA: Association for Supervision and Curriculum Development.

Perrone, V., editor. (1991) *Expanding Student Assessment*. Alexandria, VA: Association for Supervision and Curriculum Development.

Wiggins, G. (1992) "Creating Tests Worth Taking." *Educational Leadership*. 49, 8:26-33.

_____. (1991) "Standards, Not Standardization: Evoking Quality Student Work." *Educational Leadership*. 48, 5:18-25.

_____. (1989) "Teaching to the (Authentic) Test." *Educational Leadership*. 46, 7:41-47.

Chapter Nine:

 **Teaching to the Way We Learn**

Principle 7: Strategies that represent the natural functioning of the brain will result in more significant, longer-lasting learning.

Strategies are the third component in creating a curriculum that works. They include all the teaching/learning activities, materials, resources selected by the teacher to facilitate achievement of the outcomes as demonstrated in performance of the assessments. Many factors affect the selection of strategies including students' abilities, rate of learning, learning styles, readiness, interests, experiences, culture; teachers' abilities, training, experiences, learning styles, culture; availability of resources and materials; number of students in class and physical space; the learning outcomes and the assessments. Following the approach to curriculum development in this book, the last two factors provide the starting points and context within which other factors operate as refinements in the selection process.

Strategies must relate first and foremost to outcomes and assessments. Teachers must select them precisely in relation to how well they are likely to promote the intended learning. If the outcome has to do with the acquisition and integration of declarative knowledge, teachers will select strategies that help students construct, organize, and store knowledge. These may include such things as helping students experience content using a variety of senses, teaching them to use the K-W-L strategy (what do students *K*now, what do students *W*ant to know, what will students *L*earn), providing advance organizers, helping students create physical and pictographic representations of information, presenting and practicing linking strategies, and so on. If the outcome has to do with acquiring and integrating procedural knowledge, teachers will select strategies that let students "walk through" the new skill (think aloud demonstrations, flow charts, written steps), will find ways to demonstrate the skill and engage students in practicing it, and will help them set up practice schedules for long-term learning.

If the outcome has to do with developing critical thinking skills, teachers will ask questions that require the thinking skill, give examples, present steps for students to use when engaging in a particular kind of thinking, provide graphic organizers for using the skill with specific content, have students practice with teacher-structured tasks, and then further engage them in student-structured extending activities using the particular thinking skill. **Figures 9.1** and **9.2** offer two ways of classifying a variety of strategies related to the purposes of learning or teaching.

If the outcome in tandem with the assessment asks students to create a product or performance, instructional strategies will include combinations of those used to teach needed knowledge and skills, along with presenting models/exemplars, establishing and communicating criteria, providing opportunities for teaming and collaboration, and developing student self-assessment skills.

Not all strategies fit a given outcome. Strategies for storing information do not suffice for learning a skill; strategies for acquiring a skill do not suffice for meaningful use of the skill in a real-life context. At the same time, many different strategies are appropriate for helping students acquire knowledge; many different strategies are appropriate for acquiring a skill, and so on. From among the strategies that match the kind of learning identified in the outcome and demonstrated in the assessment, teachers select some on the basis of other factors such as students' learning styles and modalities, culture, age, experience, and so on. The **first** principle of strategy selection, then, involves matching strategies with the learning outcome; the **second** principle matches strategies with the kinds of assessments used to demonstrate learning; the **third** principle aims at variety as the most likely way to assure addressing the individual differences among learners. Underlying all these principles of selection, however, is the fundamental reality of how the brain works, how learning occurs.

Figure 9.1

Teaching Strategies

The following strategies are illustrated in ASCD, *Teacher's Manual for Dimensions of Learning*:

I. Acquiring and Integrating Knowledge

Declarative Knowledge

Constructing Knowledge

1. Three–minute pause
2. Experience content through senses
3. K–W–L strategy
4. Concept attainment process
5. Reciprocal teaching techniques
6. Before, during, after strategy
7. Brainstorm and predict
8. Metaphors and analogies

Organizing Knowledge

1. Physical and pictographic representations
2. Graphs and charts
3. Organizational patterns and graphic representations
4. Advance organizer questions
5. Note–taking strategies, including graphics

Storing Knowledge

1. Symbols and substitutes
2. Link strategy
3. Formal systems
4. Rehearsal
5. Mnemonics

Procedural Knowledge

Constructing Models

1. Thinking aloud demonstrations
2. Written set of steps
3. Flow charts
4. Mental rehearsal
5. Analysis
6. Analogous skills and processes

Shaping Skills or Procedures

1. Demonstration and practice of variations
2. Error analysis
3. Situational use
4. Interviews with experts

Internalizing Skills

1. Practice schedule
2. Charting accuracy and speed

II. Extending and Refining Knowledge

1. Questioning
2. Comparing: examples, steps, graphic representation, comparison activities
3. Classifying: examples, steps, graphic representations, classification tasks
4. Induction: examples, general strategy, graphic representations, induction outings, trasnslating facts into generalizations, probabilistic thinking, induction matrix, whodunits, author's intention, hidden assumptions
5. Deduction: examples, general guidelines, deductions from specified generalizations, categorical arguments, graphic representations, conditional arguments
6. Error Analysis: examples, general strategy, finding errors in declarative and procedural information, distinguish fact and opinion, common biases, informal fallacies, rewrite faulty argument
7. Constructing Support: examples, general strategy, ways of developing a persuasive argument, components of well–structured appeal to reason, argument analysis
8. Abstracting: examples, general strategy, graphic representations
9. Analyzing Perspectives: examples, general strategy, value examination matrix, conflict clarification matrix, situational analysis, current events

III. Using Knowledge Meaningfully

1. Decision–making: examples, model of steps, tasks, application to life–situations, pictographic representation
2. Investigation: examples, steps, tasks, graphic representation, community applications
3. Experimental Inquiry: examples, model of steps, tasks, graphic representations
4. Problem Solving: examples, model of steps, tasks, graphic representation
5. Invention: examples, model of steps, tasks, analogies, graphic representation

IV. Habits of Mind

1. Self Regulation: examples, strategies and techniques, long-term goals, process observers, positive reinforcement
2. Critical thinking: examples, strategies and techniques, debate, reinforcement, process observers
3. Creative thinking: examples, strategies and techniques, structured problem–solving, reinforcement, process observers

Outlined from Robert Marzano, et al, *Dimensions of Learning* (Teacher's Manual), ASCD, McRel, 1992.

Figure 9.2

Teaching Strategies

Preparation Techniques

These techniques are designed to prepare students for new learning, new information by bringing forward students' prior knowledge and experience and by attaching that knowledge and experience to the new learning situations.

Brainstorming	Circle of knowledge
Concept–mapping	Interpretation of data
Chaining/webbing	Corners
Kindling	Interviewing
Do–look–learn	Case Studies
Metaphorical learning	Simulation games
Inductive learning	Learning centers
Know–Want–Learn (KWL Method)	

Presentation Techniques

These teachings are designed to present students with new information. A presentation lesson usually follows a preparation lesson and is organized in terms of a few key concepts, topic and sub–topic.

Storytelling	Concept description
Peer–reading	Lecture
Jigsaw	Demonstration
Compare & contrast	Lab experiments
New American lecture	Field trips
Advanced organizers	Oral reports
Concept attainment	Written reports
Venn diagrams	Inquiry
Clustering	Analogies
Know–Want–Learn	T–Charts
Metaphorical lecture	Modeling
Inductive learning	Resource people

Process Techniques

These techniques provide opportunities for students to work with information, to inquire about its causes and effects, to apply it to new contexts, to use it to create new concepts and generalizations and to analyze its structure.

Think–pair–share	Interviews
Teacher speaks–student summarizes	Oral reports
	Role playing
Continuum	Classifying
Round table	Sequencing
Categorizing	Predicting
Group discussion	Visualizing
Three–step–interview	Analogies
Key word tactics	Inventing

continued on next page

Figure 9.2 continued

SQ3R	Associating relationships
Peer problem solving	Modeling
Concept mapping	Simulation games
Carousel brainstorming	Inquiry–discovery
Compare and contrast	Guided instruction
Reading for meaning	Discourse–synthesis
Debates	
Panel discussions	

Practice Techniques

These strategies are designed to make the retrieval of information easy and automatic. Students need to work actively with new information and be provided with speedy feedback.

Boggle	Making analogies
Proceduralizing	Computer–assisted instruction
Peer practice	Team game tournaments
Trading problems	Quizzes
Pair check	Games
Send–a–problem	Rhyming
Graduated difficulty	Acting out
Concept mapping	Funding patterns
Inductive learning	Mnemonics (Acronyms, etc.)
Reading for meaning	Outlining
Compare and contrast	Metaphorical review

Guide for the Writing of Curriculum, Archdiocese of Chicago

Figure 9.3

True or False

1. The brain is better equipped to handle complex
   input than simplified data. _____
2. All learning is experiential. _____
3. Threat inhibits learning. _____
4. The part of the brain that controls emotions also structures cognition. _____
5. Learning that follows the natural processes of the brain
   is easy and enjoyable. _____
6. Most students forget 50% of the information recalled on tests. _____
7. The number of possible interconnections in a single human
   brain is greater than the number of atoms in the universe. _____
8. Brain–compatible learning will always have a creative component. _____

(Key: 1.T; 2. T; 3. T; 4. T; 5. T; 6. F (85%); 7. T; 8. T)

We know that the brain is the organ for learning. Just as we would not allow a heart surgeon to operate without knowledge of how the heart functions, or an ophthalmologist without knowledge of how the eye functions, so should we insist that educators know enough about how the brain works to create and sustain brain-compatible learning environments. **Figure 9.3** offers a simple true/false quiz as a way of gauging a faculty's current understanding of brain-functioning as it relates to the teaching/learning process; it also serves as a springboard for input and discussion.

The resources listed at the end of the chapter offer more extensive information about brain-based teaching and learning. Working from the items in **Figure 9.3**, I would like to highlight some key principles of brain-compatible education to keep in mind when selecting strategies to match outcomes and assessments in a curriculum that works.

The brain is designed to use lots of *input* to build *patterns of action* to accomplish *goals*. This picture of the brain presents educators with some serious realities to take into account when planning instruction.

The brain is better equipped to handle complex input than simplified data—complex, not confusing. The principles of clear organization in presenting new material still apply; however, the notion that isolated, oversimplified nuggets of information or skill must precede active engagement with a larger context does not apply. In a brain-compatible learning environment, for example, students learn grammar in the context of communication, rather than primarily in the context of worksheets and drill and practice. Students learn scientific information not simply to recall it on tests, but in the context of problem-solving and relation building. They learn basketball in the context of playing the game; vocabulary in the context of communicating about, not just memory; historical facts in the context of significance. A curriculum that articulates *significant* learning in *outcomes* makes it easier to support and maintain instruction that respects the learner's natural need for rich and complex context.

All learning is experiential. Learning means I take input through the senses to *form* (discover)/*build* patterns which I use to *act* in my environment, in the situation. *I* have to do it; a teacher cannot do it for me, cannot give it to me ready-made. A lecture, by itself, offers a weak teaching tool precisely because it represents someone else's conclusions. A learner finds lecture helpful only to the extent the learner can connect what's being said to his own experience and use it to build new patterns. The less experience a learner has in an area, the more teachers must supplement lectures (and textbooks) with active, hands-on learning opportunities. Even prestigious graduate schools find the case study approach tremendously effective in facilitating more integrated, expert knowledge and skill.

Threat inhibits learning. If I'm building new patterns, I have to feel safe or I will revert to what already feels comfortable or safe. Threat is not the same as concern or disequilibrium. Socrates' old admonition, "To learn one must first know what she does not know," remains true. A good teacher creates situations that challenge the learner to try something else, perhaps precisely because it has become clear that what worked before won't work now. Handled well, this sets up exactly the kind of imbalance that motivates learning. What shuts down inquiry is the threat or fear of physical or psychological harm. A brain-compatible learning environment will make room for mistakes on the way to learning without irreparable negative consequences too soon. Grading every attempt at a complex performance will discourage risk taking. Over-insistence on conformity with the teacher's preferences limits creativity. Sarcasm and verbal abuse undermine confidence, as does extensive failure. Brain-compatible teachers will doggedly safeguard against setting up classrooms and structuring learning experiences that students perceive as truly threatening.

The part of the brain that controls emotions also structures cognition. All learning has an emotional component. When teachers tap into it positively, they deepen the learning. On the other hand, negative feeling tone in the classroom blocks new, long-lasting learning. Teachers using brain-based strategies work to set up a positive climate and to engender positive attitudes toward the learning tasks.

Learning that follows the natural processes of the brain is easy and enjoyable. The brain is always active; it is designed to learn. We do not have to motivate human beings to learn, although we may need to motivate students to learn what we are teaching now. Because of the way the brain works, learning should be satisfying, even when it requires hard work. When students announce that some part of what they are learning is boring, dumb, meaningless, perhaps they are right. These represent real feelings that probably signal that the learner is not engaged; and the learner must be engaged to learn. High levels of student involvement and purposefulness, along with the relative absence of strain and tension, mark brain-compatible learning situations.

Most students forget at least 85% of the information recalled on tests. When students learn information in order to reproduce it on a test, they retain and transfer little of it once it leaves short term memory. Brain-based educators speak of two kinds of memory: taxon memory and locale memory.

Taxon memory has to do with one-to-one matching, with what we call rote memory. It takes a tremendous amount of attending to do this, requiring the brain to limit the number of simultaneous input channels in use. Locale memory, on the other hand, lets us take in and store information situationally, using multiple senses in a context involving emotions and purpose. It is the difference between memorizing a route to the art museum in a strange city and experiencing the city enough to use a map to get to the museum from wherever you are. The brain's natural functioning is more akin to the dynamic of locale memory than taxon memory. Knowledge learners have *used* stays with them longer, can be retrieved more easily and is acquired more happily.

The number of possible interconnections in a single human brain is greater than the number of atoms in the universe. Two compelling implications flow from this revelation. One, the human brain is immensely powerful, yet we often communicate extremely limited expectations for learning for many students. Two, to some degree, learning will always be individualized. Students *can* learn what we have to teach; we must find multiple ways to give them the room to learn it for themselves in their own ways.

Brain-compatible learning will always have a creative component. Learning means pattern-building, connection-making. Each *learner* builds the patterns and makes the connections for himself. Even though we have studied the same subject matter, using the same resources, the learning in my brain is different from the learning in your brain in real ways, based on the uniqueness of our prior experiences and learning. Brain-compatible learning acknowledges and makes room for the unique expressions of learning that come from each learner. Teachers apply criteria in common; the performances are unique.

To sum it up, classrooms and instructional situations that respect how learning occurs naturally will be increasingly characterized by these descriptors:

active, active, active

experiential

multi-sensory

reality-based

purposeful.

Figures 9.4 and **9.5** provide two additional, striking summaries of brain-based learning at work.

In using the principles of brain-based learning to structure the teaching/learning process, educators need to adopt three key perspectives:

1. Student as *doer*, not receiver.
2. Teacher as *coach*, not dispenser of knowledge.
3. Learning as building *patterns of action*, not a collection of right answers (isolated skills and facts).

In general, this means that teachers need to:

1. Talk less.
2. Engage students more actively.
3. Use real life situations and experiences.
4. Allow more choices.
5. Reduce threat to help students take more risks.

Figure 9.6 provides a list of student products teachers might find helpful in designing learning activities and assessments.

A curriculum decision-making process that invites schools to identify significant learning outcomes, design authentic assessments for students to demonstrate the learning, and select teaching/learning strategies to facilitate performance of the significant learning as demonstrated in the assessments, provides a strong structure to support brain-based education. Given what we know about how the brain works, *significant learning outcomes* represent learning that is more brain-compatible; and this significant learning will be better facilitated using brain-compatible teaching and learning strategies. Just as the kinds of assessments teachers use shape the learning achieved, the kinds of *strategies* teachers use shape the learning achieved. When outcomes are significant and assessments and strategies are designed and used to match the outcomes, we will have a curriculum that works. **Figure 9.7** diagrams the match among outcomes, assessments, and strategies in a way that includes the rich overlay of significance in learning outcomes, authenticity of assessments, and brain-compatibility of strategies.

Figure 9.4

... a child in a passive classroom
dominated by standard seatwork tasks
experiences brain deprivation.

What do students do in democratic brain-based learning classrooms? They initiate and plan projects, research problems, work in small teams, generate reports, prepare charts and graphs, use media and tools, create poems and stories, produce skits and plays, conduct community studies and surveys, write newspapers, invent and deliver real products or services, teach, tutor, intern and work with mentors.

This all adds up to a foreign but vital aspect of brain based learning environments—emotion. Emotion resides deep in the brain and rational thought. Brain-based learning engenders satisfaction, delight, pride, and joy. When you generate that spirit in the learning response, you are on the right course to brain based learning environments. Learning that is MEANINGFUL, EMOTIONAL, and energized with frequent opportunities for APPLICATION results in easy, natural and indelible learning. Students enrolled in brain-based schools of learning learn many times more than before.

Experiential education at its fundamental
level means students shape what happens.

Wayne B. Jennings, *Brain-Based Education Networker*, Fall, 1989. Volume I, Number 3.

Figure 9.5

What We Know

1. Intelligence is a function of experience (not genetics). Experience sparks the development of brain dendrites. Dittos do not make dendrites! Nor do textbooks used as a sole source in the classroom. Learning must be active and experiential to spark dendrite growth.

2. The brain is a pattern–seeking device and is not naturally logical and sequential. In order for brain patterns to develop, input in the classroom must be meaningful, enriched and of real life.

3. Most useful knowledge is stored as part of a program (mental structure for applying information). Students need the latitude to manipulate information in their minds, to have multiple and frequent opportunities to communicate about and apply knowledge, skills and values.

4. In order to learn, students must avoid down–shifting from the cognitive area of the brain. The environment must be free of threat, real or perceived threat (e.g., not belonging or being liked by their peers). There must be trust, choices and adequate time.

Susan Kovalik and Karen D. Olsen, *Brain–Based Education Networker*, Fall, 1989.

Figure 9.6

The A–B–C's of Student Products

A
Advertisement
Advice column
Album
Allegory
Ammonia imprint
Amusement party
Anagram
Anecdote
Animation
Annotated
  bibliography
Announcement
Anthem
Apparatus
Application form
Art gallery
Artifacts
Associations
Audio tape
Autobiography
Axiom
B
Baked goods
Ballet
Banner
Batik
Beverage
Bibliography
Billboard
Biography
Blueprint
Board game
Book
Book cover
Box
Brochure
Budget
Building
Bulletin board
Business
Business card
C
Card game
Cartoon
Campaign
Carving
Case study/case
  history
Catalog
Celebrity cards
Ceramics

Charcoal sketch
Charts
Checklists
Choral reading
Cinquain
Classified ad
Clothing
Club
Code
Collage
Collection
Comedy
Comic book/strip
Community action
  service
Computer program
Conference
Convention
Cooperative game
Costume
Course of study
Crossword puzzle
Crocheting
D
Dance
Debate
Demonstration
Design
Detailed illustration
Diagram
Diary
Diorama
Directory
Discovery
Documentary
Doll
Drama
Drawing
E
Editorial
Embroidery
Energy saving device/
  plan
Equipment
Essay
Estimate
Etching
Eulogies
Experiment
F
Fable
Fabrics

Fact file
Fairy tale
Family tree
Fantasy
Fashions
Feature story
Field trip
Film
Filmstrip
Fiction
Flags
Flannel board story
Food
Formulas
Furniture
Future scenarios
G
Gadgets
Gallery
Game
Game show
Garment
Gauge
Gift
Glass cutting
Glossary
Graph
Graphic design
Greeting cards
Guest speaker
H
Haiku
Handbook
Hats
Headlines
Helper service
Hieroglyphics
Histories
Hologram
Horror show
Hotline
I
Icons
Identification charts
Illustrated story
Index
Inscription
Insignia
Invitation
Instrument
Interview
Inventions

J
Jamboree
Jazz
Jewelry
Jigsaw puzzle
Jobs
Joke
Joke book
Journal (personal,
  scientific)
Journal article
K
Kaleidoscope
Keepsake
Kit
Knitting
L
Labeled diagram
Labels
Laboratory
Ladder of ideas
Languages
Latch hooking
Laws
Layout
Learning center
Leatherwork
Lecture
Legal brief
Lei
Lesson
Letters (inquiry,
  complaint,
  personal, etc.)
Letter to editor
Library
Limerick
Line drawing
List
Lithograph
Log
Logo
Lyrics
M
Machine
Macrame
Magazine
Magazine article
Magic trick
Make–up

continued on next page

Figure 9.6 continued

Map
Marquee
Masks
Meetings
Menu
Mobile
Model
Monologue
Monograph
Montage
Monument
Mnemonic device
Movie
Mural
Museum exhibit
Museum
Musical composition

N–O
Needlework
Needs survey
Newsletter
Newspaper ad
Newscast
News story
Notice
Novel
Novella
Oath
Observance
Observatory
Observation record
Occupation
Oil painting
Opera
Opinion
Oral report
Oration
Orchestration
Organization
Original
Outline

P
Package for a product
Painting
Pamphlet

Pantomime
Paper weight
Papier mache
Park
Parodies
Patterns
Pennants
Petition
Photo essay
Photo file
Photographs
Picture book
Picture dictionary
Pillow
Plan
Play
Poem
Pop–up book
Poster
Pottery
Prediction
Press release/
    conference
Prototype
Puppet
Puppet show
Puzzle

Q
Quarterly report
Query
Question(s)
Questionnaire
Quilting
Quilt
Quiz

R
Radio Program
Rank ordered list
Rating
Reaction
Reader's theater
Recipe
Relief map
Research report
Resolution

Review
Riddle
Robot
Role playing
Rubbing
Rug hooking

S
Sand casting
Satire
Scale drawing
Science fiction
Scientific theory
Scrapbook
Sculpture (soap, metal,
    clay, junk, wire)
Set/scenery
Short story
Silk screen
Simulations
Skit
Slide show
Slide/tape presentation
Song
Song book
Sonnet
Speech
Sport
Stained glass
Stencil
Stitchery
Store
Store display
Story
Story telling
String art
Stuffed animal
Survey

T–U
Tape recording
Taxonomy
Television program
Term paper
Terrarium
Test

Text book
Theme
Theory
Tie–dyeing
Timeline
Tool
Tour
Toy
Transparencies
Travel brochure
Travelogue
Trip
Uniform
Unit of study

V
Variety show
Vehicle
Verse
Video game
Vignette
Visual aid
Vocabulary list
Volunteer program

W
Walking tour
Wall hanging
Wallpaper
Watercolor
Weather map
Weaving
Whittling
Woodwork
Word games
Written report

X–Y–Z
Xerographic print,
    collage
Xylographics
Yarn (story)
Yearbook
Yodel
Zodiac
Zoographic studies
Zoological projects

List compiled by: Donna R. Mahr, Educational Consultant, 561, N. Main St., Oregon, WI 53575 (608) 835–9830

Ideas borrowed from: Engine–Unity, Product List for Independent Study. Feldhusen & Treffinger, The *A–B–C's of Student Products,* Home–school learners, WPA Conference, 1989–90.

Figure 9.7

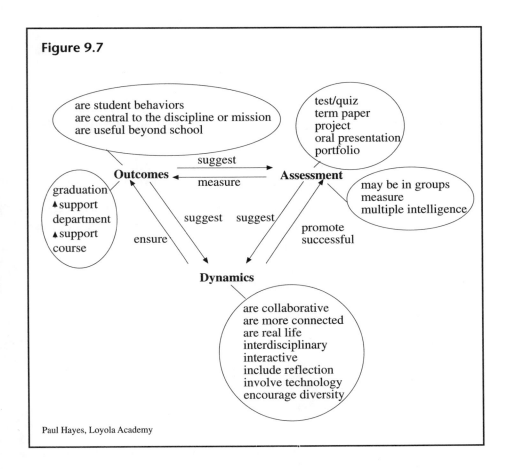

Paul Hayes, Loyola Academy

Selected Resources

Archdiocese of Chicago, Office of Catholic Education. (1990) *Guide for the Writing of Curriculum.*

Brain-Based Education Networker. Published by The Institute for Learning and Teaching. 449 Desnoyer, St. Paul, MN 55104-4915.

Cane, Renate Nummela and Geoffrey Cane. (1991) *Making Connections: Teaching and the Human Brain.* Alexandria, VA: Association for Supervision and Curriculum Development.

Engine-Unity, *Product List for Independent Study*, Feldhusen & Treffinger, *The A-B-C's of Student Products,* Home-school learners, WPA Conference, 1989-90.

Gardner, Howard. (1983) *Frames of Mind: The Theory of Multiple Intelligences.* Basic Books.

Hart, Leslie. (1983) *Human Brain and Human Learning.* Village of Oak Creek, AZ: Books for Educators. P.O. Box 20525.

_____. (1992) *"Anchor Math."* Village of Oak Creek, Arizona.

Books for Educators.

Johnson, David W. and Roger T. Johnson. (1984) *Circles of Learning.* Alexandria, VA: Association for Supervision and Curriculum Development.

Kovalik, Susan. Susan Kovalik and Associates, Integrated Thematic Instruction. Discovery 2000. Village of Oak Creek, AZ

Mahr, Dolna R. Educational Consultant, 561 N. Main Street, Oregon, WI 53575. (608) 835-9830.

Marzano, R.J., D.J. Pickering, D.E. Arredondo, G.J. Blackburn, R.S. Brandt, C.A. Moffett. (1992) *Teacher's Manual Dimensions of Learning.* Alexandria, VA: Association for Supervision and Curriculum Development.

McCarthy, Bernice. (1980) *The 4MAT System.* Oak Harbor, IL: Excel, Inc.

Chapter Ten:

 ## Addressing Religious Education and Values Formation in the Curriculum

Principle 8: *All* **areas of the curriculum, including religious education and values formation, benefit from outcomes-centered curriculum decision-making.**

All the principles of creating a curriculum that works apply equally to developing curriculum for religious education and values formation. A worry Catholic educators often raise in this area of the curriculum centers around the reality that religious education—including evangelization and catechesis—is meant for the long run, the *really* long run. The best long-term measure of success in this area, we often argue, rests in a voluntary and grace-supported personal acceptance of a set of beliefs that inform action. We want our students to be saints. How can we capture such life-trans-forming learning in outcomes statements, much less measure achievement and evaluate it? To the extent we cannot, we cannot and will not be doing our job as professional educators.

If we are to *consciously* engage in evangelization and catechesis, then we must know what successful evangelization and catechesis look like in the response of children and young people *along the way*, not just when they have embraced the faith in ways that are fully active, conscious, and living. If the religious education program includes message, community, service, and worship, then it is our job to do the same things in these areas that teachers in other disciplines must do to create a curriculum that works: 1) define the desired learning (outcomes), 2) find ways for students to demonstrate that it is happening (assessments), and 3) select those strategies most likely to promote the learning.

We are beings who come to learn and grow and shape ourselves in community—our whole selves: spiritual, emotional, intellectual, physical. What we know, what we can do, what we are like appear in our responses to the environment, to all the situations in which we find ourselves. What we know about what someone else knows, can do, or is like, comes from what we observe. The observations may come to be so subtle, so quick, so expert that we sometimes call them intuition, but they are observations nonetheless.

The primary expertise of educators lies in the ability to apply knowledge and skills accurately and effectively to the creation of safe situations in which significant learning occurs. To the extent that educators cannot identify the significant learning and clearly determine whether or not it is occurring, to that extent they teach blindly. Furthermore, if educators cannot identify clearly when and whether significant learning occurs, it is virtually impossible for them to consciously and accurately *create* a learning environment in which learning occurs. In order to facilitate learning *professionally*, we must identify what learning we are after, what it looks like in learners when it happens, and what effect and connection a variety of strategies, responses, and experiences have on helping it happen. This is the fundamental responsibility of all professional educators, including religious educators.

Granted, religious educators may have a more difficult time with these tasks precisely because learning in this area involves choice and personal orientations which are moral and character defining. No knowledge is entirely neutral because persons use it for purposes which reflect values; however, knowledge developed in religious education programs in Catholic schools takes on a formational dimension that catapults us into outcomes, assessments, and strategies that must reflect affective as well as cognitive learning almost always. Most educators are even less adept at formulating and assessing affective learning outcomes than they are at working with cognitive ones. We tend to think of outcomes and assessments as quantifying and limiting. To create effective religious education curriculum, we must shift our mindset about outcomes and think of what we do as an opportunity to assess *all* the learning we value and thus take responsibility for it.

Using the approach to curriculum presented in this book for religious education will give us tremendous leverage not only in increasing learning for more students, but also in communicating with the various publics from whom we seek support: clergy, parents, parishioners, students. When we can articulate significant religious education learning in terms of student outcomes, and design multidimensional assessment tasks that allow students to demonstrate the learning in authentic ways, then we can see how effectively our strategies and materials are working, and we can do more of the same or change them. We will also develop more realism. Perhaps there are some things related to faith development that we cannot do in schools because our students have not lived long enough. Then let's not pretend we can (which goals encourage us to do) and let's not think we are evaluating what we cannot do. As long as we allow religious education curriculum to remain fuzzier than other parts of the educational program, we open ourselves up to wishful thinking on the one hand and much less powerful learning on the other. The challenge facing us is to discipline ourselves to articulate significant learning outcomes in religious education and then find ways to validly assess the learning so we can get the feedback needed to help it happen better for more students. In building religious education curriculum, we often begin with goal statements similar to those in **Figures 10.1** and **10.2**, or a profile statement similar to **Figure 10.3**. These can be moving and useful statements in setting direction and tone; they communicate much about the fundamental approach to religious education embraced by the community. However, as a basis for answering the three key questions for creating a curriculum that works, they remain too fuzzy to provide much help. **Figure 10.4** presents a set of PreK-12 outcomes for religious education in Catholic schools, developed by an inter-diocesan task force of seven dioceses belonging to the Supervision, Personnel, and Curriculum (SPC) division of the National Catholic Educational Association. These outcomes translate the directional, philosophical thrusts of the goals and profile statements into broad statements of what students should be able to do as a result of religious education in Catholic schools. The outcomes reflect the four areas identified in *The Religious Dimension of Education in a Catholic School*: message, community, service, and worship. Because these outcomes tell us what *students will do*, they provide the beginnings of criteria for the rest of the curriculum decision-making process: how will we know and what can we do to help it happen for all children. Working from these outcomes, individual dioceses and individual schools can use the curriculum decision-making process outlined in this book to create a religious education curriculum that works.

Figure 10.1

Religious Education Goals: K-6

- Child will grow in ability to witness to Scripture and Catholic teachings.
  —demonstrate knowledge and understanding of Scripture and teachings.
  —respond to Scripture and teachings in every day behaviors.

- Child will grow in a desire to respond to the needs and rights of others.

- Child will mature in recognition of self as a child of God, trusting in His unconditional love.

- Child will grow toward active participation in the faith community.

- Child will mature in a personal relationship with Jesus.

- Child will understand that the journey of faith is a life-long process.

- Child will be guided in the development of Christian values to aid in moral decision making process.

Diocese of Lafayette-in-Indiana

Figure 10.2

Religious Education Goals: 7-12

Adolescent Catechesis should recognize and respond to the need of youth to:

1. Possess an acquaintance and interaction with Scripture, Doctrine, and Tradition.

2. Develop a knowledge and love of Jesus resulting in a closer relationship with and witnessing to Jesus.

3. Assume responsibility for their ongoing conversion.

4. Demonstrate their ability to be church.

5. Possess love of and trust in church.

6. Grow in full membership in the community through the sacramental life.

7. Grow in moral decision making reflected in the light of Catholic faith.

8. Grow in acceptance of self as a child of God experiencing His unconditional love.

9. See the challenge of faith in a variety of life-styles within religious, single and married vocations.

10. Recognize and turn to the family as the primary catechist.

Diocese of Lafayette-in-Indiana

> **Figure 10.3**
> ### Religious Education Profile of a Graduate
>
> - Growing confidence and ability to freely discuss their beliefs in God.
> - Firm belief in God's unconditional love.
> - Recognition of self as a child of God.
> - Openness to change but able to appreciate and understand traditions.
> - Willingness to witness Christ-like values as revealed to us in the Bible and Tradition.
> - Active involvement in the preparation and participation in liturgical celebrations resulting in a true appreciation of them.
> - Growing in knowledge, understanding, and reverence for Scripture, Doctrine and Tradition.
> - Experience of and appreciation for many forms of prayer.
> - Desire to invite Jesus into everyday life.
> - Willingness to be actively involved in the parish community.
> - Developing process for moral decision making in light of their Catholic Faith.
> - Respect for life.
> - Understanding of justice and peace with a desire to work toward this way of life.
> - Appreciation of cultural and religious differences.
> - Respect of individual differences of others.
> - Active response to the Sacraments.
> - Desire to share time, talents and treasures in response to the needs and rights of others.
> - Recognition of responsibilities as stewards of God's creation.
> - Understanding that the journey of faith is a lifelong process.
>
> Diocese of Lafayette-in-Indiana

Let's walk through the process with the first of these K-12 outcomes. Students will read, interpret, and apply Scripture to life. The first step might be to identify some key, enabling outcomes that further specify the areas of learning to be assessed in the global exit outcome. (In the language I have been using, graduation outcomes and subject area outcomes represent exit outcomes; course or grade level/cluster outcomes and unit outcomes represent enabling outcomes. From a broader perspective, we might also think of subject area outcomes as *enabling* graduation outcomes.) The task force specified five such assessment categories for this outcome: read and recall

Figure 10.4

PreK-12 Outcomes for Religious Education
of Catholic Children in Catholic Schools

1.   Read, interpret and apply Scripture to life.

2.   Present a reasoned rationale, based on faith and knowledge, for being a Catholic.

3.   Illustrate basic understanding of Catholic dogma and doctrine in light of the Catechism for the Universal Church.

4.   Demonstrate the importance of Sacraments, with an emphasis on the centrality of the Eucharist, in the life of Catholics.

5.   Make moral decisions consistent with Church teachings.

6.   Illustrate basic understanding of the history of the Church.

7.   Acknowledge and affirm the diverse cultural expressions of Catholicism.

8.   Apply Catholic principles to interpersonal relationships (e.g., family, peers, work, society, church, etc.).

9.   Demonstrate an appreciation for faith community as the way we come to know God.

10. Use effective community building skills in relating with others.

11. Critique societal structures in light of Catholic social justice principles and apply these principles to societal and personal situations.

12. Engage in service to the community (e.g., family, parish, local, national, global) in response to the Gospel call.

13. Exercise responsible stewardship for the gift of creation.

14. Examine the variety of Christian lifestyles as ways to respond to the Baptismal call to a life of service.

15. Demonstrate the relationship (e.g., through arts, social sciences, science, technology, etc.) between faith and culture.

16. Use appropriate resources (e.g., Lectionary, Lectionary for Children, Scripture, Directory for Masses with Children, Liturgy Training Publications, etc.) to plan and participate in liturgy and other prayer experiences.

17. Use a variety of prayer forms (e.g., traditional, spontaneous, devotional, multicultural) to enrich and express personal and communal spirituality.

18. Celebrate the presence of the Sacred in experiences of sacramentals, symbols and rituals.

19. Demonstrate an understanding of the liturgical seasons and feasts.

SPC Region 7 Task Force on Religious Education Outcomes, 1994

Bible stories; use historical/critical method of interpretation of Scripture; locate specific information within the Bible; use Scripture for prayer and liturgy; transfer ideas from Scripture to daily life. These outcomes (exit and enabling) tell us that the curriculum we design must give students opportunity to demonstrate these learnings in age-appropriate authentic ways, working with designated subject matter, using instructional strategies that coach successful performance.

As a next step, we might agree upon subject matter to be used in demonstrating the broad outcomes at various grade/cluster or course levels. One such sample appears in **Figure 10.5**. Next we might develop grade level/cluster and course outcomes that connect the specific subject matter to the exit outcome and enabling assessment category outcomes. **Figure 10.6** presents sample grade level outcomes for grades three and seven; **Figures 10.7** and **10.8** provide sample course outcomes for a high school course on Hebrew and Christian Scriptures respectively.

Working from these grade level/ and course outcomes, then, local school educators would build a curriculum that supports a match among these broad outcomes, assessments that give children and young people valid opportunities to demonstrate the learning stated in the outcomes, and strategies that promote successful performance. Through units within a grade level or course, teachers specify the subject matter in greater detail and formulate unit outcomes, assessments, and strategies that promote achievement of grade level and course outcomes.

The same K-12 outcomes (based on Church documents interpreted by expert religious educators) can form the basis for the religious education curriculum in all the schools in the diocese. And at the same time, local educators can design unique curriculum for their schools using the parameters set by the exit outcomes. Local curriculum might specify subject matter sequenced in a different order; specific assessments might reflect local resources; teaching/learning activities will reflect student learning styles, culture, and special needs and interests. However, since the learning stated in the local outcomes is designed to promote the broad assessment category outcomes and K-12 outcomes, a school can rest assured that the learning specified is significant. Further, when local educators use these outcomes to design valid assessments and then select teaching/learning activities and materials in light of the intended performances, they can be confident that the local curriculum fits not only the school but larger standards.

Figure 10.5

Sample Subject Matter Sequence

Outcome: Read, interpret and apply Scripture to life

Kindergarten: Selected Bible Stories

Grade One: Selected Bible Stories

Grade Two: Selected Bible Stories

Grade Three: Apostles, Beatitudes, Parables

Grade Four: *Old Testament*—Overview
New Testament—Gospels

Grade Five: *Old Testament*—Prophets, Commandments
New Testament—Gospels, Letters, Corporal and Spiritual Works of Mercy

Grade Six: *Old Testament*—Key people: Abraham, Moses, David, Isaiah, Jeremiah; Key events - Passover, Exodus, Covenant
New Testament—Life of Christ in Gospels, Early Church

Grade Seven: Jesus and the Gospel Message

Grade Eight: Paul and his letters, Acts of the Apostles

High School: Hebrew Scriptures
Christian Scriptures

Figure 10.6

Sample Grade Level Outcomes

Grade Three

Students will:

1. Locate, read, and recall parables and explain them in their own words.
2. Illustrate each of the Beatitudes and give examples of practicing them in their own lives.
3. Find Scripture references to the Apostles and explain their relationship to Jesus.
4. Participate in prayer services using the parables.

Grade Seven

Students will:

1. Identify Jesus' mission and teaching as presented in the Gospels.
2. Trace the main events of Jesus' life in the New Testament.
3. Formulate a personal meaning of being a disciple of Jesus.
4. Interpret Jesus' stories from the Gospels and apply to his/her own experience.
5. Use the Gospels for prayer.

Figure 10.7

High School Course Outcomes

Hebrew Scriptures

This course deals with God's plan for humankind as manifested through the Hebrew Scriptures. Students will explore and discover contemporary and traditional ways of interpreting events in the Hebrew Scriptures and their relevance today. Students will conduct an examination of the religious, literary and historical importance of the scriptural accounts and make application to current daily life.

Students who complete the course will:

1. Analyze the way in which the Hebrew Scriptures illustrate the history of the Jewish people from a religious interpretation.
2. Examine and interpret the messianic prophecies as an intellectual framework for understanding Jesus the Christ.
3. Contrast and compare the literal and contextual interpretations of the Bible.
4. Discuss ways in which the Bible was formed and grew from a religious, historical and literary perspective of the Hebrew people.
5. Relate the significance of the Hebrew Scripture teachings and the Ten Commandments to elements contemporary to modern life.

Gordon Technical High School, 1993

Figure 10.8

High School Course Outcomes

Christian Scriptures

This course emphasizes the true impact of the Resurrection on personal spirituality as well as the collective faith and teachings of the Christian community throughout the history of the Church. The course examines the Good News of the divine becoming human and through Christ, extending membership in the "People of God" to all races and nations.

The Religious Education Department focuses instruction so that students who complete the course will:

1. Integrate a relationship between personal conduct and social accountability.
2. Use Scripture to identify examples of personal and social sin.
3. Use the Gospels and critical resources to interpret the work of Jesus Christ in the quest for truth, human rights and peace throughout the world.
4. Demonstrate a relationship between the work of Jesus on earth and the necessity for human understanding and cooperation.
5. Discuss and analyze the Call of God to our working for the full use of our human potential.

Students will examine and evaluate the life and message of Jesus Christ as it was recorded through the early Church community and interpreted by Biblical scholars.

Gordon Technical High School, 1993

A critical difference between this approach to curriculum development and following a textbook series to determine scope and sequence is that we identify and prioritize significant learning in relation to specific subject matter *in terms of the integrative outcomes* (referred to as assessment categories or enabling outcomes): read and recall Bible stories, use historical/critical method, locate information, use Scripture for prayer, transfer ideas to life. These key outcomes continually provide the basis for inclusion and exclusion of content, assessments, strategies. When we are true to this approach, no one piece of knowledge, information or skill takes on a life of its own. All are part of a rich and complex process that leads to clearly articulated significant learning that is central to the discipline, useful beyond school, leading to more learning, connected to graduation outcomes.

Figures 10.9 and **10.10** offer two additional ways of articulating integrative outcomes for religious education. **Figure 7.4** (page 90) in Chapter Seven articulates a set of outcomes consistent with *The Religious Dimension of Education in a Catholic School.* As in other areas of the curriculum, outcomes such as these form the foundation for creating a religious education curriculum that works, but they do not constitute the curriculum in and of themselves. Connections among outcomes, assessments, and strategies remain as important here as in all other areas. Consider **Figure 10.11** which outlines the curriculum for a unit in fourth grade religion. This particular statement of outcomes, assessments, and strategies indicates a learning environment designed to support and promote active, multidimensional, significant learning. Suppose we substituted these assessments for those listed in **Figure 10.12**.

Figure 10.9

Departmental Outcomes

As a result of being in the Religion Department for four years the student should be able to:

1. Make mature decisions guided by a knowledge of Catholic tradition and beliefs.
2. Identify the crippling effects of stereotypes and prejudices and apply this knowledge to social and personal situations.
3. Utilize Scripture as a source of inspiration, self–knowledge and prayer.
4. Apply the tools of biblical research to the interpretation of Biblical passages in light of modern biblical scholarship and Catholic tradition.
5. Witness his personal growth in the Christian faith by service to the local community.

Marist High School, Chicago, 1990 (Draft)

Figure 10.10

Department Of Religious Education
Curriculum Outcomes
December, 1992

The Religious Education Department focuses instruction so that students who graduate from Gordon Technical High School will:

1. Communicate the Word of God through a personal understanding of the principles of Catholic Faith.

1.1 Demonstrate a clear understanding of contemporary Liturgy.

1.2 Explain and define the concept of Church Authority.

1.3 Develop a personal style of contemporary ministry.

1.4 Explain and critically evaluate the Models of the Church.

1.5 Demonstrate a realistic interpretation of early Church issues and significant events.

2. Make informed decisions based upon a clear understanding of Catholic traditions and beliefs.

2.1 Identify and explain the various forms and purposes of prayer.

2.2 Discuss and analyze the significance of the seven sacraments as traditionally presented by the Church.

2.3 Demonstrate a clear understanding of the nature of the Trinity.

2.4 Discuss the effects of contemporary secular lifestyles on Christian morality.

2.5 Define and analyze the key concepts of Catholic sexual morality along with the personal health and social consequences of abuse and misuse of sex.

3. Interpret Hebrew and Christian Scriptures as source of greater understanding of modern social issues and contemporary life.

3.1 Define the Call of God in terms of working towards the fulfillment of human potential and talent.

3.2 Identify and extrapolate the images of God as used in Scripture.

3.3 Summarize the formation of the Bible from a religious, historical and literary perspective.

3.4 Integrate a relationship between personal conduct and social accountability.

3.5 Demonstrate an understanding of the Commandments of God and how they relate to our social and interpersonal values.

3.6 Identify examples of personal and social sin.

3.7 Interpret the concept of Goodness of Creation and human dignity.

4. Identify and distinguish the characteristics of sound moral judgment and a Christian lifestyle.

4.1 Discuss the effects of prejudice and stereotyping on human relationships and society in general.

4.2 Apply principles of Christian living through service to the community and to all in need.

4.3 Assess current issues in contemporary life and structure appropriate Christian responses.

4.4 Demonstrate the relationship between Christian marriage and the enduring strength of family values, parenting and healthy sexuality.

4.5 Construct and evaluate a personal value system in relationship to the values of Church, society and Gordon Tech.

4.6 Explain the concept of identity and relate that understanding to the issues of family and cultural heritage.

Gordon Technical High School, 1993

Figure 10.11

4th Grade Religion

Unit: Reconciliation

Subject Matter:
1. Sacrament of Reconciliation
   - Definition
   - Symbols and Signs
2. Ten Commandments
3. Examination of Conscience
4. Rite of Reconciliation

Outcomes:
1. Students will explain the meaning of reconciliation in the Catholic tradition.
2. Students will connect their understanding to their lives as active Christians.

Sample Assessments:
1. The students will write a letter to the pastor explaining why reconciliation is an important part of the life of a Catholic Christian.
2. The student will create a book of examples of people choosing to act in accord with the commandments or choosing not to.
3. With a partner students will prepare an examination of conscience which could be used with their families.
4. Working in cooperative learning groups, students will plan a reconciliation service for   the parish and explain what they did and why.

Suggested
1. Mini-presentations on theology and current practices.

Strategies:
2. Role-play of following and not following the Commandments.
3. Videos of diverse reconciliation services and discussion.
4. Interview of parish priests and parishioners about reconciliation in parish.
5. Classroom enactments.

Figure 10.12

4th Grade Religion

Sample Assessments:

1. Students will recite the Ten Commandments.
2. Student will complete the worksheet on examination of conscience.
3. Student will define the Sacrament of Reconciliation and outline the current rite for individuals.
4. Student will pass an objective test on Reconciliation, including terms, symbols and current practices.

Figure 10.13

Religious Education Outcomes Framework Guide

Outcome Statement: Read, interpret, and apply Scripture to life.

Rationale: Scripture, as a vehicle of revelation, enables Catholics to discover truth about oneself, God, others and the world.

Assessment: Read and recall Bible stories

Categories: Use historical/critical method of interpretation

Locate specific information within the Bible

Use Scripture for prayer and liturgy

Transfer ideas from Scripture to daily life

	Grade 12	Grade 8	Grade 3
Sample Assessment Tasks	Working with a Scripture study group, students identify the Sunday lectionary reading, establish the context of the story, develop three pivotal questions which link the context of the passage to contemporary life, use these questions to engage in a discussion, and evaluate the small group's discussion in light of the Sunday homily.	Student researches a Scripture citation using appropriate references to interpret the story, and translates ideas from the passage into his/her daily life.	Students work together in groups to select a Bible story to read and then present to the class through the medium of art, music, or drama.
	Student chooses a theme from Scripture and compares its presentation in Hebrew and Christian Scriptures with contemporary Church experience.	Working in groups, students use a collection of pictures from current periodicals to present the practice of each Beatitudes in today's world.	Students practice and proclaim Scripture readings during liturgy.
	Student keeps a Scripture-based journal over the course of a semester in which she/he connects the Scripture to everyday life experiences.		Students work in pairs to locate five designated Scripture passages and explain in their own words what they mean.
General Performance Criteria	Use and variety of study resources
Facility/accuracy in locating Bible passages
Aptness of translation of Scriptural concepts into modern terms
Evidence of personal reflection	Use of study resources, e.g. concordance, commentaries, etc.
Facility/accuracy in locating Bible passages
Aptness of translation of Scriptural concepts into modern terms	Bible story selected
Presentation understood by teacher/peers
Quality of proclamation
Appropriateness of interpretation

SPC Task Force, K-12 Religious Education Outcomes

The resulting classroom would most likely reflect more teacher-centered strategies focused on promoting learning at the lower end of the outcomes (recall and explanation). As with other areas of the curriculum, the most powerful religious education curriculum will begin with significant learning outcomes, will create valid and authentic assessments that give students the chance to demonstrate the learning in meaningful ways, and will identify activities and resources true to the way we learn to coach students to success.

Local schools write curriculum. Dioceses and standards committees can help by providing expert task forces to articulate exit and major enabling outcomes, and perhaps to suggest sample exemplary assessments at various points, as well as general criteria for assessment. **Figure 10.13** presents a sample framework guide which the Region 7 Religious Education Outcomes Task Force has developed for each of the K-12 outcomes listed in **Figure 10.4**. Again, the outcomes and the framework guides are not a curriculum; they provide a set of expert standards within which schools can develop local curriculum that supports the critical match among outcomes, assessments, and strategies needed to promote powerful learning.

One final word about values formation as part of the curriculum. Many schools identify specific values and character traits in their mission and philosophy. Often, these stem from the charisma of the religious congregation that staffs or sponsors the school, or the goals and priorities of the diocese. If these are to play a meaningful role in the curriculum, local schools must incorporate them into the curricular and extracurricular program by using the same decision-making process we have been examining for the rest of the curriculum: formulate outcomes, design assessment opportunities, select and use strategies.

For example, several high schools in the Archdiocese of Chicago identify service as an integral part of their missions. If this value and way of acting is truly to be a hallmark of their graduates and not just part of a well-sounding statement, local educators must make conscious choices to incorporate service into the significant learning of the school. The principles of outcomes-centered curriculum decision-making work well in making these choices.

First, we must translate "service" into student outcomes. What would students *do* who are women and men working to integrate a commitment to service into their lives? One school that used service as an affective target area in the new North Central Outcomes Accreditation Process formulated these outcomes:

1. Students will engage in at least one service project each year.

2. Students will write an annual reflection on the role of service in the life of a mature Christian.

3. Students will discuss the impact of service on themselves and their friends.

Second and third, we must develop opportunities for students to demonstrate the outcomes and select strategies to help them do it. Where in our courses and/or extracurriculars will there be service projects for students to do? When and where will they write reflections? Who will read them and give feedback? What kind of feedback? When and with whom will students discuss? How will students grow in their ability to assess their own growth in this area? How will faculty develop the knowledge, skills, attitudes and insights they need to help students in this area? The answers to these questions and others like them have the power to form a curriculum that works for values formation in service. Accomplishing these outcomes may lead to richer outcomes; shortcomings on these outcomes may lead to restructuring courses or homeroom, or advisory groups. The bottom line in this area, as in all others, rests with articulating desired learning into student outcomes. Once we have identified the responses we will call significant learning, we can go after them self-consciously. That is, we can make sure there are ways to see the learning happening; we can see if it is happening; we can do something differently if it is not happening; we can celebrate that it is happening.

I worked with a large public high school that selected ethical behavior as one of its affective target areas for Outcomes Accreditation. After a great deal of discussion among the faculty and with parents, they narrowed the focus to "taking charge of yourself." They translated this value into the following outcomes:

1. Students will greet each other civilly inside and outside classrooms.

2. Students will come prepared for class.

These two outcomes may seem relatively small when considering the whole field of "ethical behavior"; however, the school could not consciously and effectively impact "ethical behavior" until teachers, administrators and parents agreed on some specific behaviors that would constitute significant learning for these students at this time. Once they identified the specific outcomes they would address, they were able to design assessments and structure interventions that supported and coached the outcomes. They were quite successful.

None of this is to say that the only learning students engage in relating to service or ethical behavior is the learning specified in the outcomes and consciously connected to assessments and strategies. It is to say that the only learning we can claim we are taking conscious, professional charge of is the learning for which we develop outcomes-centered curriculum, implicit or explicit. If the curriculum is for all students, it must become explicit beyond one teacher.

At some point we all resist naming what we do, what we accomplish, because it often seems less in the naming than in the general sensing of it. Creating a curriculum that works puts us on the line for two things simultaneously: One, admitting that if we cannot name it, we have no real idea whether it's happening and may or may not be contributing to making it happen. In any case, we have very little wherewithal to make it happen better. Two, we must name all the learning we value, not just the easily described and measured.

All the principles of creating a curriculum that works apply equally to developing curriculum for religious education and values formation. Religious educators must do what teachers in other disciplines do to create curriculum that helps more students learn: 1) define the significant learning (outcomes), 2) find ways for students to demonstrate the learning in real-life contexts (assessments), and 3) select those strategies most likely to promote the learning.

Selected Resources

Ozar, L., D. Beaudoin, R. Bratton, T. Butler, P. Kawczynski, B. Kerkhoff, J. Landuyt, M. Lentz, J. Miller, J. Sisler. *"By their Fruits You Shall Know Them..." K-12 Religious Education Outcomes for Catholic Students in Catholic Schools.* Washington, DC: National Catholic Educational Association, 1994.

The Religious Dimensions of Education in a Catholic School. (1988) The Congregation on Catholic Education. Washington, DC: United States Catholic Conference.

Chapter Eleven:

 ## Making Outcomes-Centered Curriculum the Basis of School Reform

Writing curriculum is hard work. So is delivering it to students. It is never worth it, unless students learn and grow in ways that matter for their lives. Outcomes-centered curriculum decision-making focuses curriculum development where it belongs—on student learning. Student learning provides the starting point and the endpoint. Student learning drives assessment and instructional design. Student learning provides the touchstone of accountability and the constant source of feedback throughout the teaching/learning process.

At no point does this book present a fool-proof formula for creating and implementing an outcomes-centered curriculum. Nor does it offer *the* model of a good curriculum. To do so would be fraudulent. To be successful, local educators must come together to understand the three critical components of the curriculum and how they relate to each other. They must agree to shift the mindset from inputs to outputs and then commit to instructional planning that follows the output model: formulate outcomes, design assessments, select strategies. They must struggle together to bring values-integrating and discipline-specific learning outcomes into a set of culminating (graduation) and enabling (program/subject area) outcomes that drive course/grade/cluster and unit planning.

Local educators can use all the resources available to help them identify significant learning and state it in outcomes. They can develop expertise in designing valid and reliable assessments to match the outcomes. They can continually expand their repertoire of teaching/learning activities to promote successful performance of the learning stated in the outcomes. In the end, however, they must discipline themselves to make some choices, put them on paper, and teach what they have chosen as a school.

We release the full power of outcomes-centered curriculum to increase learning for all students only when we do it *together*, consistently and over time, in a school. And that is virtually impossible unless we write it down and then use what we've written as the basis of daily/weekly planning. The most difficult part is the beginning. Writing the curriculum will remain hard, painstaking work, but it can move apace with professional energy and even excitement once the faculty establishes a common vision of where they are headed and why. The primary purpose of this book has been to help in the formation of that vision by articulating a framework in which the critical components of the educational process come together to increase learning.

We can look at the educational process as a *system* in which several key components interact to increase or decrease learning. **Figure 11.1** offers a graphic representation of this system, adapting Peter Senge's "Limits to Growth" archetype. The left circle in the diagram represents the growth cycle. As educators, we embrace increased learning (achievement) as the fundamental goal of education. What are the factors that positively impact increased learning? Certainly, a clear vision of intended, significant learning (outcomes), along with appropriate and effective teacher interventions (strategies). The more significant the outcomes and the more effective the strategies, the greater the learning.

The right circle represents the limits to growth in this system: assessment. No matter how significant the stated outcomes, the quality and nature of the achieved learning is most directly shaped by the quality and nature of the assessments. Outcomes may call for integrative, higher-order learning; teachers may conduct class sessions that encourage critical and creative thinking. Yet, if the assignments and tests essentially require reproducing information and practicing relatively isolated skills, the quality and extent of the learning will decrease. Whereas, when the assessments match the integrative, higher-order learning outcomes, they will drive more dynamic, appropriate teacher interventions to increase and expand the quality of learning.

A good written curriculum offers a road map to teachers to help them keep the system in a growth cycle. This means addressing the connections among outcomes, assessments, and instruction. Focusing on any one component alone will not result in a curriculum that works because it ignores the critical synergy among the parts of the system that promotes long-lasting growth.

Outcomes-centered curriculum decision-making, as outlined in this book, provides such a map. When used by a school, such a curriculum will not only increase learning, it will also serve as a catalyst for school renewal and reform. Once a school declares the significant learning it will promote and commits to aligning assessments and strategies to help it happen, it sets the parameters for other areas of decision-making. Faculty, administrators, boards, parents can begin to ask: Is the day organized in the best ways to promote the learning? Is there room for enough communication across subject areas? Do our policies and procedures support students' practicing and developing the characteristics and qualities identified in the graduation outcomes? Do we allocate resources in ways that reflect the learning priorities? Do role descriptions and responsibilities of teachers, administrators, and support staff contribute to our students' achieving the outcomes? Does the physical plant support the learning as well as it can? And so on. In all these areas, *student learning* will guide decision-making.

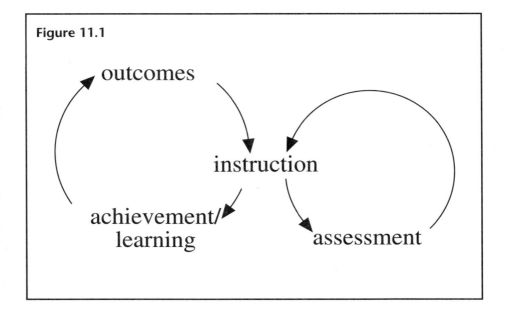

Figure 11.1

One final comment about resources. Certainly, resources are a contributing factor in the educational process. I deliberately left them out of the system diagram in **Figure 11.1**. There is another system archetype Senge talks about called "Shifting the Burden." In this model, we try to fix the system (improve results, increase growth) by focusing our attention on achieving a symptomatic solution rather than identifying and going after the fundamental solution. Increasing resources by itself can easily become a symptomatic solution that distracts our energy from the more fundamental solutions. Fantastic materials can be a marvelous asset in promoting dynamic teaching and learning. Higher salary scales can attract better teachers. Students from higher socio-economic backgrounds with more highly educated parents can be better prepared to achieve higher scores on standardized tests. Attractive buildings in safe neighborhoods can more easily generate happy learning communities. It can, but may not.

Resources contribute to a curriculum that works to the extent that the educators responsible for the curriculum use them to articulate significant learning, design authentic assessments, and select appropriate strategies. While a certain level of absence of resources will constrain the process, their presence will not guarantee results. Even more, creative, committed teachers and administrators can use outcomes-centered curriculum decision-making to achieve more learning for more students in the face of very limited resources.

Every educator dreams about calling forth more learning from more students. Because we are professionals, we can and must use knowledge and skill to consciously create learning environments in which this happens everyday for every student. Outcomes-centered curriculum decision-making offers a powerful and proven approach to turning the dream into a reality.

References

Senge, Peter M. (1990) *The Fifth Discipline: The Art and Practice of the Learning Organization.* New York: Doubleday Currency.